Guy

CRIN ME

Some situations really make you want to crawl into a hole, don't they? Here are a few pet "cringes" sent in by readers:

Don't you just cringe when:
You try on a skirt that's too tight, and the zip gets caught in your tights and you have to ask the assistant for a pair of scissors!
Fiona, Aberdeen.

Your little brothers have just conned you into playing with them, and you're in the process of chasing t
and mak
the hunk
walks by
though y

You're bopping away at the disco, and your mate subtly mentions that the coloured mousse you thought had styled your hair beautifully is now sitting in a great orange blob on the top of your head!
Karen, Kent.

GAME, SET AND MATCH!

Our neighbour is always borrowing things, and usually manages to get the things he wants. He put on his best performance ever the other day, though.

"Are you mowing this afternoon?" he asked Dad, over the fence one day.

"Yes," said Dad quickly, afraid that if he loaned the lawnmower out he wouldn't get it back for weeks.

"Oh, that's good," said our neighbour. "You won't be using your tennis set, then – can we borrow it?"

Dad just gave up after that!

Wham! Fan, London.

ARMY GAME

When my small brother saw a TV programme about the army, he got very excited.

"I'm going to drive a tank when I grow up!" he announced.

"Well," said Dad, "I certainly won't stand in your way!"

One of his better jokes, we thought!

Tracy, Nottingham.

BOYS WILL BE BOYS

I don't think my brother's English master will be able to stand his job much longer.

Trying to explain the meaning of the word "collision" to the class, he said,

"If two boys ran into each other, what would the result be?"

"A fight, sir?" suggested the class smarty-pants!

Cathy, Merseyside.

This great drawing of Nick Rhodes was sent in by Shirley from Manchester.

UNLUCKY 13

My boyfriend's mate is brilliant at getting people to lend him money. He's had to employ a pretty subtle approach these days, though, as people are beginning to be very wary of him.

"Are you superstitious?" he asked me the other day when we were all out together for the evening.

"No," I said puzzled.

"Oh, that's good," he said. "You won't mind lending me £13, then – I really need it!"

I'll have to think carefully when I'm talking to him, in future!

Karen, Ilford.

BROUGHT TO BOOK!

My boyfriend decided to apply for a job as a book-keeper recently, and, when I went round for tea, his family were discussing his chances of getting the job.

"I'd say he's pretty well qualified." grunted his dad, "I've known him to keep library books for years and years!"

Sharon, Kent.

IT'S A DRAW!

We're Star

Find out what 87's got in store for you with our great star guide...

CAPRICORN

(Dec 23-Jan 20)

You probably found that the last twelve months brought you lots of personal luck. Everything you said or did worked out really well, and you'll be feeling on top of the world by now.

But the good luck is still around, and in the next year it's to be found in the *money* area of your chart.

Expect windfalls. Negotiate for more spending money, or an increase in wages at work. You'll get most of what you ask for, and you could find that everything you touch turns to gold. That's great news for Capricorns, because you're one of the most money-minded of all signs, usually earning it by very hard work, but no luck. This is the big lucky year!

AQUARIUS

(Jan 21-Feb 19)

Are you ready for this? Probably! Being an Aquarian you're used to the unexpected, good or bad. But, being an Aquarian and just a little suspicious, you might think that this year sounds too good to be true. It isn't. This is your year, Aquarius.

You'll have so much personal good luck that you'll get even more of that famous Aquarian glow. Trust to luck, for once. It's really on your side!

PISCES

(Feb 20-Mar 20)

All your luck this year will be behind the scenes. There'll be things going on that are being planned for your benefit, and being a Pisces, and rather psychic, you'll probably sense that things are somehow turning in the right direction, at last.

Your finely-tuned instincts about things and people are touched by luck this year, and you could do well to trust to hunches. You'll have been more lucky through insights, and by the end of this year you'll find that some of your feelings about those close to you have been proved to be right on course. This is the year to train your intuition. Start an astrology course.

ARIES

(Mar 21-Apr 20)

This is the year your social life gets its lucky break, and you could find yourself in a new and exciting group of friends, or the old mates will suddenly decide that they need you to be the life and soul of their party.

You'll be a sensation at the disco, or on the sports field, and when there's a minor crisis in your private life, your mates will rally round to help.

Go for meeting new people, and your Jupiter luck will make you sparkle.

TAURUS

(Apr 21-May 22)

Taking exams this year, or applying for a job? If so, hold on to your hat, because this is the year that everything works out much better than expected on the career front.

That should make you feel a lot better, after the last disastrous eighteen months. Something you do in the next twelve months will earn you the respect of everyone around you, which should be great news for Taureans, who like respect even more than they like dossing.

You're going to have to work a bit harder than usual, but the work will produce fantastic results.

GEMINI

(May 23-June 21)

Luck's with you on your travels this year. This summer could bring you the holiday romance you've always dreamed of, and even if Romeo doesn't emerge from the sea on the very first day, all the other ingredients of a holiday of a lifetime will still be there – sun, fun and *no* complications. You could also strike lucky if you make some attempt to get on a higher education course. Aim for the stars as far as your education is concerned, because they're well within your reach.

CANCER

(June 22-July 22)

If you work in a bank, Cancerians, or in insurance, or anything where you handle money, expect a promotion at work. As for *most* of your luck – this is a bit difficult – but if one of your relationships has been stuck because you've been a bit shy, you won't be this year.

No more playing wallflower and gooseberry! Some guy is going to decide that you turn him on to boiling point. No, it doesn't sound like your usual experience at all, but when luck strikes, who's arguing?!

LEO

(July 23-Aug 22)

This is the year you could start a love affair that could last for ever. With Jupiter aspecting your chart from Aquarius, the traditional prediction of the next twelve months is that it's the year you could get engaged or married! There won't be many enemies around you, at any rate, and someone is going to offer you undying love and support. Take it while it's going. It isn't often that you get such a good year for forever romances.

87

ry Eyed

VIRGO

(Aug 23-Sept 22)

If you're unemployed, Virgo, luck's on the side of job prospects, this year. Someone is going to pick you out as the perfect employee, and finally recognise your potential for organising and reliability.

And there's a big bonus for Virgo health, this next twelve months. Don't worry about putting on weight – you could well gain a few pounds. Just thank your lucky stars that you feel on top of the world, and on top of all your troubles, and enrol on a fitness course. You'll glow with health and security!

LIBRA

(Sept 23-Oct 22)

This next twelve months your love-life takes off into the stratosphere. No, it's not the Real Thing, but it's good things, one after another.

You'll be able to attract more or less any guy you fancy, and you'll fancy quite a few! You'll be happier than you've been for a while, as far as romance is concerned, and if you're a creative type, interested in making a name for yourself in art or writing or music, this is the year when creative luck is with you, too.

So go out and *make* something happen!

SCOPRIO

(Oct 23-Nov 21)

You've got some very heavy planets lying on you at the moment, but Jupiter in Aquarius should at least mean that some of your burden is lightened quite a bit.

You'll start getting on quite well with your parents in the next twelve months, and your home life should improve dramatically because of this. There'll be fewer rows, and there could be a stroke of real luck at home which will mean that everyone's in a great mood, and willing to put up with your glooms and joke you out of them.

SAGITTARIUS

(Nov 22-Dec 22)

You won't have the same kind of dramatic luck as some of the other signs, but you should find life lightening for you in lots of small ways.

You'll be able to come across to others more easily, and perhaps someone who's been missing from your life will reappear magically.

Or you could finally meet a guy you've been writing to for a long while.

Anything to do with letter-writing or making telephone calls, or acting, is going to be lucky for you this year. So write off, now, for your application form for drama school!

– will you be in Heaven?

CHATTING UP BLOKES REQUIRED NERVE, TACT AND SUBTLETY!

Amy wanted to make the first move – so Caroline told her...

DON'T MAKE IT OBVIOUS

Caroline was giving Amy some advice.
WHATEVER YOU DO, DON'T MAKE IT OBVIOUS, THEY **HATE** BEING PROPOSITIONED.
She was the type that **loved** giving advice.
YOU THINK SO?
CHATTING FELLAS UP IS EASY AS LONG AS YOU CAN JUDGE WHAT THEIR REACTION'S GOING TO BE. THE REALLY TIMID ONES LOVE YOU BEING FORCEFUL WITH THEM.
. . .BUT THE MACHO TYPES CAN BE VERY SUSPICIOUS. YOU HAVE TO PRETEND IT'S THEM CHATTING YOU UP, EVEN THOUGH **YOU** KNOW IT'S THE OTHER WAY ROUND.
AND OF COURSE, THERE'S THE SLEAZY TYPES WHO THINK JUST BECAUSE A GIRL'S MAKING THE FIRST MOVE SHE MUST WANT ONE THING.
WHAT DO YOU DO WITH THEM?
DISAPPEAR TO THE LADIES LOO FOR HALF AN HOUR AND WAIT TILL THEY'VE GONE.
SO, WHAT DO YOU THINK YOU'RE GOING TO DO WITH BILLY?
I HAVEN'T A CLUE. I'M NOT EVEN SURE THAT'S HIS NAME.
BECAUSE HE WORKS IN A RESTAURANT, I THOUGHT I COULD BUMP INTO HIM OUTSIDE WHEN HE COMES OFF SHIFT.
OH NO, COME ON. IS THAT OBVIOUS OR WHAT? YOU'VE GOT TO BE STYLISH, SHOW HIM YOU'RE CONFIDENT. ASK HIM IN THE RESTAURANT.

"I can't Caroline, I'll chicken out."

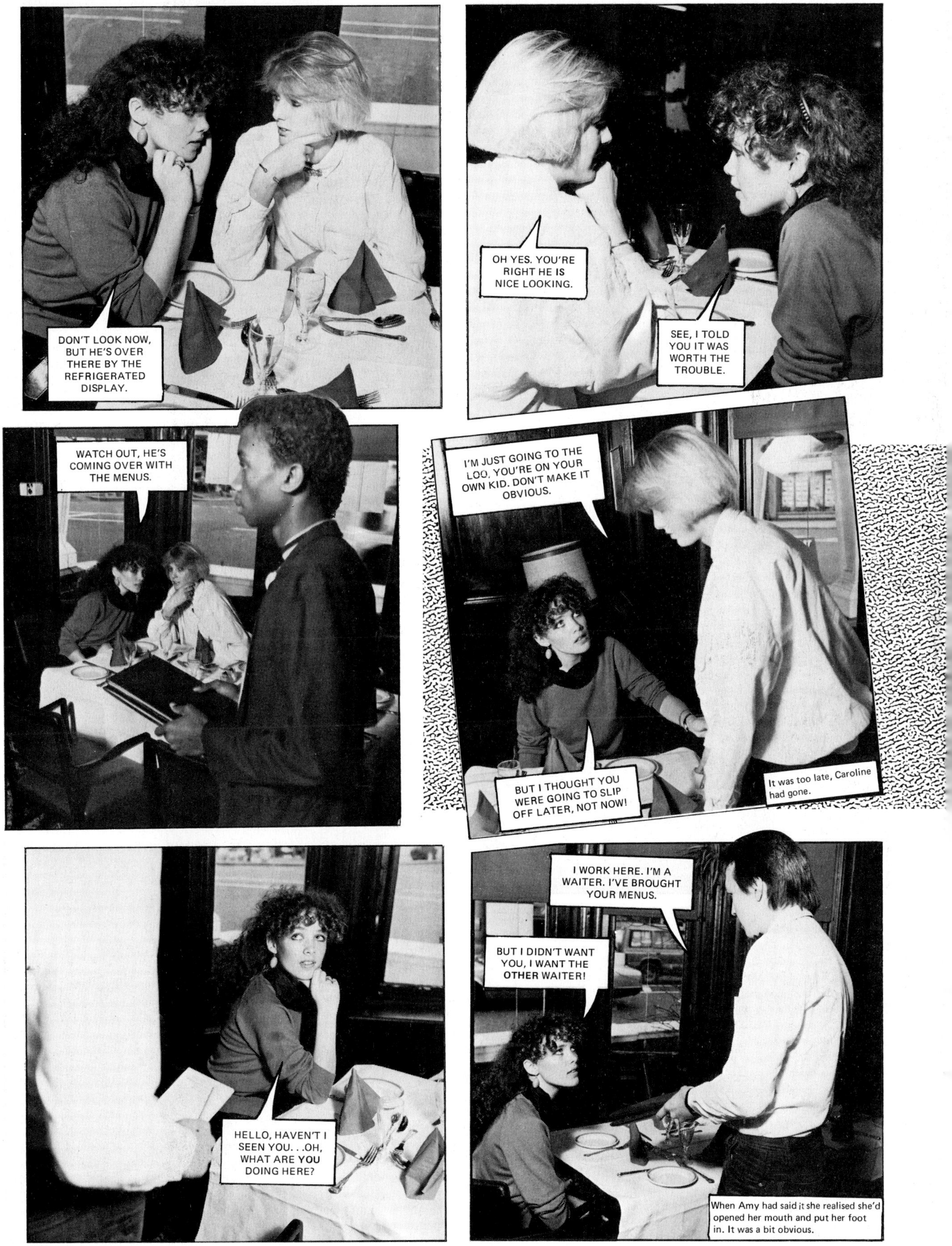
DON'T LOOK NOW, BUT HE'S OVER THERE BY THE REFRIGERATED DISPLAY.
OH YES. YOU'RE RIGHT HE IS NICE LOOKING.
SEE, I TOLD YOU IT WAS WORTH THE TROUBLE.
WATCH OUT, HE'S COMING OVER WITH THE MENUS.
I'M JUST GOING TO THE LOO. YOU'RE ON YOUR OWN KID. DON'T MAKE IT OBVIOUS.
BUT I THOUGHT YOU WERE GOING TO SLIP OFF LATER, NOT NOW!
It was too late, Caroline had gone.
HELLO, HAVEN'T I SEEN YOU. . .OH, WHAT ARE YOU DOING HERE?
I WORK HERE. I'M A WAITER. I'VE BROUGHT YOUR MENUS.
BUT I DIDN'T WANT YOU, I WANT THE OTHER WAITER!
When Amy had said it she realised she'd opened her mouth and put her foot in. It was a bit obvious.

"We've got that other creep."

When the bill came it was Billy that brought it.
HERE'S THE BILL, MADAME.
OH, THANKS.
I CAN'T LOOK AT HIM, I'LL GO RED.
DOG & FOX

But on the back of the bill was his name and a phone number.
HE'S LEFT HIS PHONE NUMBER FOR ME.
BILLY
5729

When she looked up he was watching her.
IT'S WORKED! AND I DIDN'T HAVE TO SAY A THING!

Their eyes did all the talking.
YOU SEE, TO BE HONEST, I DIDN'T THINK WE STOOD MUCH OF A CHANCE. I DIDN'T WANT TO TELL YOU THAT BEFOREHAND BECAUSE I WANTED TO KEEP YOUR CONFIDENCE UP.

NEXT TIME WE COME, WE'LL HAVE TO PLAN WHERE WE SIT MORE CAREFULLY.
YES, CAROLINE.
LITTLE DOES SHE KNOW THERE DOESN'T HAVE TO BE A NEXT TIME.

AND REMEMBER THE GOLDEN RULE. DON'T MAKE IT OBVIOUS!
IF ONLY SHE KNEW.
THE END

The funny side of love!

Does loving and losing break you up?

Well, does it? Right from the first moment when you look at him, and he looks at you and your mate whispers, "Is he squinting or are you cross-eyed?", it's hysterical. And then there's the beautiful part when you're sure it's the Real Thing, and your earring gets stuck in his new perm as you whisper, "I love you," in his shell-like ear.

Or his earring gets stuck in your new perm.

Finally, we come to the tragic end, that last goodbye, when you tell him it's all over, and keep looking at your watch to drop a hint that it's time he gave you your hanky back, because your new guy's waiting for you outside the ABC.

You can take it seriously if you like, but isn't it more fun to look at the funny side of love?

And if it breaks you up, why not break into giggles? Sob with laughter. Crease up, don't crack up. Forget about the broken heart, think about the belly laughs.

Eye to Eye Contact

"My first big 'romance' was with Pete, our milkman. You know, I was up at a quarter to six every morning, in the bath, hair wash, full make-up, best clobber, hanging around casually in our front garden by quarter to seven, waiting. He'd come along, plonk down our milk, drop me a meaningful wink, and that was it, my big moment for the whole day. Then I'd have to go in, change into school uniform, wash the make-up off and crawl into school, half dead with exhaustion and excitement. Wow! I lived on those winks for a whole month, before I started wondering if it was really worth it."

Michelle, Berkhamstead.

Come on, you've done that, too. Well, maybe not exactly that, but done the same amazing dressing up act for the one you love, hoping to catch his eye. We've all gone mad with the blusher and mascara to go on a bike ride past *his* house, so don't be embarrassed.

"Every night, when I came out of work, I used to see this wimpy bloke at the bus-stop. Eventually, we'd sort of nod to each other. In the end, I realised that no matter what time I came out of work – five o'clock, half past, even six, the same guy was still waiting for that bus, still nodding to me. So I walked round a corner, and watched him. Sure enough, he walked away from the bus-stop, got on a motor-bike that had been parked by the side of the road, and rode off. He'd just been waiting there to see me. It's touching, really, but it's

Famous First Lines

"I met this boy at a party. Well, I sort of looked him over, and he looked me over, too, and I was melting deliciously inside, so I moved over, and said, "Who's the most beautiful deaf girl in the world?" It was a joke of the time. He was supposed to say "Who?" and then you said "What?" and he said "Who?" again, and you said "What?" Pathetic really. But this guy, this luscious guy, happened to be deaf, really and truly deaf in one ear, the ear I murmured into. So the chat up went, "Who's the most beautiful deaf girl in the world?" "What?" "What?" "What?" "What?" "What?" We must've whatted for about five minutes before I realised what was happening. It was really embarrassing!"

Julie, Liverpool.

Not all first lines are embarrassingly funny. Some are just funny funny. But none of them are good enough to pass the Great Moments of My Life test when you think about them. They're always good for a giggle.

dead funny, isn't it?"

Janine, Huddersfield.

That famous eye-to-eye contact, then, the first big signal of 'How about it?' that gives you the tingles in your toes and multi-coloured stars in your line of vision, can be the start of a funny game, or the opener of a side-splitting joke. Not at the time, of course. Then, as you begin to fall in love, you're not playing for laughs. You honestly believe that you're playing for keeps. But think back to *your* first move in your last romance. Isn't it just a little bit funny?

Harsh Words

Aren't they? Look back at some of the laughs in your rows. Lovers' rows are probably the funniest rows of all.

"Paul and I went on holiday to Spain last year with his parents. He's scared of flying, and that made him really picky, even before we arrived at the hotel. Then he accused me of chatting up this other guy on the coach from the airport, and started sulking. So, after I'd unpacked, I went into his room and started bawling him out for being childish. He called me some names, so I picked up his case, and threw it our of the window. It dropped straight into the hotel swimming pool! Only it wasn't his case – it was his dad's! That wasn't exactly the happiest holiday of my life, but I do laugh about it now."

Jane, Walthamstow.

It's a good test of whether your love's going to last if both of you can laugh your way through these rows. And it's a good test of whether or not you're completely over him if you can look back at that final sad goodbye, and smile at that, as well…

The First Kiss

And then there's the first real moment of pure magic when lips meet and… Have you ever thought about why wonderful things happen when two mouths push themselves against each other? Scientifically, it's got something to do with nerve-endings, and blood vessels, and scent hormones, and chemical reactions. Personally, it can have the effect of your very own internal November the fifth, especially if you've been kissed by a red-hot guy. But it's a funny business, isn't it? Lining up your mouths so your noses don't collide, especially if you pull away at the last moment to spray your mouth with deodorant.

"We'd been in a crowd, all night. Finally, we got off the bus together, outside my house, and waved goodbye to all our mates. It was a still, starry night. Beautiful. He leaned towards me, touched my cheek with his fingertips, and I stood on tiptoe and leaned into him. He said "Kathy… here!" and handed me this spiky false eyelash that had fallen on to my cheek. Great!" ***Kathy, Rotherham.***

"He just pulled me towards him, and kissed me, long and lovingly. It was totally unexpected. So unexpected that I swallowed my chewing gum, and choked for the next five minutes." ***Nicola, Peterborough.***

No, honestly, you shouldn't laugh at something as perfectly romantic as a first kiss. But, on the other hand, why not? At least you can get some enjoyment out of it, even if it was a total failure. What about the first big row, though? Rows are never funny. Are they?

The Punch Line

It might seem strange but saying that last goodbye can be funny, as well as painful. Sometimes, it's such a relief, after weeks and weeks of holding on, or trying to make the best of a bad situation, that a good giggle's more appropriate than a thousand wet tissues.

"Nick had been cheating on me for weeks with one of my friends. I knew about it, but for ages I fooled myself that I could get him back. When I decided it was time to give up, I called round at his house on a night I knew he was supposed to be seeing her. I did the full tragic act, taking back all his letters, and all the things he'd bought me, and howled all over him for three hours, telling him I'd realised he didn't love me any more. Of course, I didn't tell him that I knew he was two-timing me.

"I just forced him to do his big sympathetic and tearful bit, consoling me, and pretending to be as miserable as I was. It was a lovely scene, that goodbye. And I got all the more enjoyment out of it, thinking about her waiting for him in the carpark for three hours!" *Rebecca, Oldbury.*

Revenge can be very sweet. But even the really tear-jerking final scenes can have their funny moments.

"We kissed, one last time, in his car. He said, 'Sorry, Angie, it just doesn't mean anything any more'. I felt as if my heart had stopped beating. I said, 'I'd better go, then'. He said, 'Yeah, you'd better'. I climbed out of the car, and stood there, really breaking my heart while he leaned out of the car window, said, 'See you around', and went to drive off. But the car wouldn't start. I stood shivering and sobbing on the pavement.

"He sat cursing in the car, trying to get the engine to turn over. In the end, I had to stop crying, and help him push the car."

Angie, Wisbech.

Somebody once said that laughter is very close to tears.

So why don't you, instead of crying your way through a crumbling romance, play it for the laughs, instead? Let's get some enjoyment out of this strange thing called love.

It's the greatest two-some comedy turn there's ever been!

MIRROR MIRRO

WHICH IS YOUR S

you

Go on – which is the about? Or – put it is the bit you hate reveals the hidden Read on... And when your own secrets, your fella's too...

Y O U

EYES

A dreamer.
This girl has her feet planted firmly in the world of make-believe. Romantic fiction, films with happy endings, fairy tales with handsome princes – she can't get enough of them. And that's why real life romance proves disappointing! Each time she gets to know the REAL bloke – he ups and turns into a frog. She needs to grow up.

FACE

Is it her fortune?
This girl believes she's wonderful! And expects everyone else to think so too. Fellas – who she treats to an occasional well-practised-in-front-of-the-mirror smile – are chosen for who they are – not what they are. She doesn't waste time with any old Tom, Rick or Gary. She's a social climber. But she's destined to take a tumble.

HAIR

She's hiding.
However outrageous the style, a girl who believes her hair is her crowning glory is very insecure.

Each change of style, colour or length emphasises a mood change and a desire for disguise.

She uses her hair to attract fellas – but has no faith in her abilities to keep them interested.

BREASTS

She's the tops.
If a girl's happy with her bust – she's happy with life. It doesn't matter whether they're 30A or 38D – it's quality, not quantity. She's sexy, lively and brimming with self-confidence. Not surprisingly, her warm and friendly personality attracts fellas in droves.

BACK

One of the lads.
She's strong, brave and one of the boys. She's got no time for feminine wiles. She speaks her mind and expects others to do the same. She doesn't want to be the boss – or be bossed. Fellas must be her equal. But if you need a shoulder to cry on – you can rely on her to provide sympathy and the solution.

BOTTOM

Not prepared to take a back seat.
This girl needs to be the centre of attention. And her tight jeans and skirts usually ensure that she is. Watch her wiggle and giggle. And then watch the fellas watching her. They can't keep their eyes off her – or her rear – and that's just the way she planned it. But she'll break their hearts. Being faithful? She doesn't know how to!

LEGS

She'll never walk alone.
Although more than capable of handling life alone, this girl will never get the opportunity. She's such fun that she's always surrounded by both blokes and girls.

She's independent and very capable of getting exactly what she wants.

ON THE WALL –

XIEST BIT OF ALL?

it you feel best
another way – which
east?! Your answer
ou. Fascinated?
ou've discovered
ave fun finding out

him

H I M

EYES

Watch them melt.
One look from his smouldering eyes is all it takes to get the girls. Or so he believes. Like his female counterpart, he's been watching too many films.

But things have changed. Real girls like real men. If he's to stand a chance of success – he's got to come down to earth with the rest of us.

FACE

Not just a pretty one.
A guy who believes in his face gets people to believe in him too. He's open, honest and incredibly nice. He's generous with his smiles. And he's not just flashing them at pretty girls. He's popular with both sexes because he doesn't present a threat to his mates. They know they can trust him.

HAIR

Everything to lose.
A guy who's in love with his hair is revealing even greater insecurities than the girl who worships hers. The reason? He's scared stiff of losing it. As a bloke, he knows he stands a good chance of receding hairlines or – even worse – going bald. Consequently, he's nervous, uptight and unsure of himself.

Poor lad. Someone should tell him that baldies are rumoured to be the best lovers.

CHEST

Puts on a good front.
Whatever the temperature, the first glimpse of sun and it's off with his T-shirt. Mr Macho himself. Stand back and admire him, girls. Because that's just what he wants and expects. He's a super-confident show-off who uses girls to adorn his right arm. But he doesn't waste time on anyone less than stunning. It would be bad for his image.

BACK

Someone to lean on.
This guy's a man's man. Okay, he may take a passing interest in girls – he may even have a girlfriend. But she'll come a poor second to the real loves of his life – football, knocking back the pints or a night out with his mates. He's strong and dependable and confident he'll make it to the top of whatever career he chooses.

BOTTOM

A real asset.
This guy knows what turns a lady on. And he exploits his rear with well-cut designer jeans. He falls in love and out again at breakneck speed. But beware – once he falls in love for real, it's forever. He's possessive, jealous and definitely the boss.

LEGS

He's a good sport – physically and emotionally. And he's great fun to be with because he doesn't take himself seriously. His best jokes are always at his own expense. But, deep down he really does need to be admired. But like his legs, he keeps this side of his personality hidden.

The Bond Between

They grew up together, went to school together, formed a band together, stayed together. And now, after eight years, still Spandau Ballet's solid bond grows stronger every day.

Eight years is a long time for any band to stick together, but the five who make up Spandau Ballet have always been close, ever since their uniform upbringing in Islington, North London.

Born within two years of each other, Tony Hadley, John Keeble, Steve Norman and brothers Gary and Martin Kemp all went to Owen's Grammar School, all had the same working class background, and all were friends from an early age onwards. So it was natural that they should want to do something together upon leaving school and sporadically joining the dole queue.

And so it was in 1979 that they became an overnight success, as the spearhead of the New Romantic movement, a faction moving in direct opposition to the previous headliner, punk, and one which was to spawn **the** sound of the Eighties.

Spandau Ballet couldn't have had a smoother initiation to stardom, with debut release *To Cut A Long Story Short* peaking at number 5 in the charts.

Since then they've not looked back, and have come a long way since those raw beginnings when they could barely call themselves 'musicians' let alone show off any prowess to anyone else.

In fact, in their embryonic stages, Steve hadn't even so much as held a bongo drum let alone play the sax, while Martin was more keen on a career with Arsenal and had no musical ability whatsoever. Tony, though, was pretty much an old hand, having been winning talent competitions from the age of 13 onwards.

"I think that gave me confidence to think I could get into show business. I've always been a bit of a show-off anyway and I never really contemplated doing an ordinary job. I know that sounds ambitious but I just didn't," he explains.

"I think my parents were a bit worried when I told them. The first thing they thought was, 'Is he going to turn posh?' Second, 'Is he going to get involved in drugs and things like that?' And thirdly, 'is it all going to go to his head?'

"Before I joined Spandau, I took any job that was well-paid, so I could spend all my money going out and having a good time with my friends. But when it looked like we could have fun *and* be successful with a group, I never thought twice about giving up my job.

"You have to stick your neck out and take chances or you'll miss out on a good time."

MATES

Spandau make it a policy never to have anything **but** a good time, as Steve is quick to point out. "Enjoyment comes first. But then, I had fun when I was on the dole, before the money and all the acquisitions. I don't see this as a job. What's more, we're all real mates. If I fell out with the band, I'd be out of friends. We actually do get on."

"And we don't parody the way a rock star 'should' act," says Gary.

Adds John, "We've still got our feet firmly on the ground. People always say your attitude changes when you get famous, but it's usually people's attitudes to *you* that changes. If I see kids from school, people I knew fairly well, they don't know how to approach me. It's strange.

"But the best thing about the band is that my best mates are all in it, so it's not a problem."

Steve agrees. "Once, we'd been on tour and then spent time promoting an album until we were like zombies at the end. So we had about a month off, away from each other. But I was only away for a few days when I thought, I want to get back to my mates."

So, they're undeniably close to each other, but you'd have thought maybe there'd be some kind of friction within the band, especially between the Kemp brothers – family intolerance and all that. Apparently though, it works to their advantage.

Gary explains. "It's very easy for me and Martin to argue. We've been arguing since we were small, and because we're brothers we can say anything to each other, call each other what we like, without hurting our relationship.

"We tend to take sides purposely to vent arguments about which direction things should go in the group, which otherwise might get out of hand.

"We can talk about anything together because we got on so well. It's hard to explain, but my relationship with my brother is spiritual. I could never have a friend who would be as close to me as Martin. We wouldn't have the same parents or share the same love. I don't have to tell Martin things, and vice versa. I also can't argue with anyone the same way as I can argue with him.

"Sometimes we can get so angry with each other, we even fight physically, but it'll all be over and forgotten in five minutes. If there's a disagreement in the band, Martin and I take sides and fight it out between ourselves, because we have the kind of relationship which can take it."

When you think about it though, all the lads could just as easily be brothers. They're all so alike, with the same attitude to life, their work, and each other. And even when they're no longer playing in a group, it'll be that bond called love that will keep them inseparable.

The Ballet Boys

What's kept them so close?

TEARS FOR
FEARS
MYGUY

BILLY IDOL
MY GUY

FASHION VIC

Dressing up in style should be fun, not a headache. So, make sure you're not a victim of fashion by reading our cheap chic guide.

Flicking through glossy fashion mags can be a depressing business when you count the cost of dressing *à la mode.*

However, do remember that fashion editors want to show you the latest trends first, and when any new design emerges onto the market, it's very often on the expensive side, simply because it's new, with high-fashion styling.

So, use your imagination, and let the fashion pages lead you in the right direction. As there are lots of different fashion themes going on at the same time, one way of cutting costs, and getting yourself a strong, well co-ordinated look, is to take a good look at all the new styles at the beginning of each season, and then decide which one best suits your looks, figure and personality. Then stick to your chosen style and build on it. This eliminates the problem of buying something then getting it home, to find none of your shoes, jackets, etc go with it.

A TOUCH CLASSICAL

Another way to cut costs is to stick to simple shapes, without fuss or frills. Choose classic shapes such as a blazer-style jacket, a simple cotton or silk shirt, a selection of jumpers and a fashionable, but still simple, pair of trousers and skirt. Choose a neutral colour scheme to work on. Fashion editors are known for dressing in black, for instance. Then build on this by adding splashes of bright colours, and add accessories to bring them more up to the minute.

ADDED INTEREST

Accessories are in fact one of the best ways to make a simple outfit fashionable and put your individual stamp on it.

Also, take a look at less obvious places. For instance, browse through the men's and even childrens-wear departments, or what about sports shops and chain stores? They often have something which corresponds to clothes in the fashion shops. And of course, second-hand shops are becoming increasingly popular sources of good buys, and some of our most innovative dressers get their gear second-hand.

Unfortunately, cast-off clothes nearly always smell musty, but once you've transported them home and into the washing machine they'll be as good as new.

Similarly, take a look in antique shops, as they often have a clothes department and they're always a marvellous source for fashion jewellery. So, be creative and you'll end up with a much cheaper and far more individual and stylish effect.

TIM

MASTER THE ART

This is the season of good will and time to party party. So, go out in style with our tips for perfect yuletide make-up and get your fair share of Christmas spirit.

MAKE-UP FOR XMAS

When putting on the Ritz, ready for the evening's festivities, make sure you make up with even lighting on your face.

Skin should be cleansed, toned and moisturised before making up, and any oiliness can be removed with a mild astringent afterwards. If your skin is spotty, you may like to wear foundation all over your face, otherwise just a little over the odd spot or blemish will suffice. Choose a foundation which matches your skin tone. Too dark, or light a shade will look false and ugly.

COVER UP

To find the right one for you, test a little on your face rather than on your hand. To cover spots and blemishes, apply foundation to these areas with a fine brush and blend well. If you want all-over coverage, follow this procedure and then dot make-up all over your face and neck, and then blend with fingertips or a slightly damp, wedge-shaped cosmetic sponge.

Apply a light dusting of translucent powder using a fat brush. Powder can be applied by itself to remove shine and give an even skin tone, on clear young skins. Blush on with blusher applied to the most prominent part of your cheekbone. To find this, try sucking in your cheeks. Use a fat brush to sweep blusher down from your hairline along the cheekbone, to stop level with the middle of your eye. Blend well, as harsh lines are unattractive.

There are basically two different eye types and make-up to suit each. Deep-set or small eyes don't have much lid showing and there isn't much space between eyelashes and eyebrow. These should be made up with dark colours at the outer corner of the eye, and lighter shades from the centre of the eye towards the nose. The other type is the protruding eye, which has a prominent upper lid. This type of eye area suits stronger colours worn in the centre of the eye, fading out into paler shades at the outer and inner corners. Use soft, matte colours on this eye type. Blend all colours well and correct any mistakes with cotton wool buds. Apply mascara and brush eyebrows into shape with a brow brush or an old toothbrush, using upward and outward strokes.

Define your eyebrows with short feathery strokes of an eyebrow pencil or dip your brow-brush in brown or black eyeshadow and brush through your eyebrows.

KISSABLE

For perfect lip colour, first outline lips with a lipbrush dipped in the colour of your choice with the excess wiped off on the back of your hand. Then fill in again with lip gloss, blot and reapply.

Using pale shades will make lips appear larger, but wearing dark shades will draw attention to them. For a perfect pout when using dark shades, apply a paler, pearly highlight to the centre of your lower lip and blend for fuller looking lips.

Now you're ready to have yourself a very merry Christmas.

TOM
BAILEY
MYGUY

THE SHOP 'N' SCREAM GUIDE!

Does a day's shopping drive you nuts? Next time you come in from a day at the sales, find your score on our rage – rating guide and find out the best treatment for yourself!

KEY
*** = mildly irritating.**
**** = very irritating.**
***** = enough to send you to a padded cell.**

Add up the number of stars from each section, then check out your score

ON THE WAY:

1. You're trapped in a jam on the bus for half an hour next to: a punk who's playing Heavy Metal loudly and tinnily on his Sony Walkman (*); a punk who's playing Heavy Metal mega-loudly on his ghetto-blaster (**); a tone-deaf lunatic who insists on serenading you loudly with "I did it My Way" (***).

2. A loose paving-stone causes you to: stub your toe (*); have two pints of cold, muddy water spilt into your new shoes (**); take a nose-dive (***).

3. A car turning into the road you're crossing doesn't bother to signal its intentions, and nearly mows you down – and the driver hoots at you as though it's all your fault (**).

IN A DEPARTMENT STORE:

1. In order to find the next down-escalator, you are cunningly forced to cross an entire floor loaded with exciting goodies, and end up spending so much that you've no money left for the thing you came out to buy (**).

2. The toilets are located on the fifth floor, take half an hour to find – and you're desperate (***). When there, you find both taps suddenly run boiling hot while you're still covered in soap, and the oh-so-hygienic hot-air drier doesn't work, so you have to dry your hands on your skirt (*).

3. Your slim heel catches in the grooves of the escalator and suddenly you're barefoot. (**).

ON THE WAY HOME YOU DISCOVER:

1. That mark or flaw in the fabric that the bad lighting prevented you from seeing in the shop (**).

2. The foil top of the yoghurt you bought as a snack has split, spreading sticky pink gunge in your plastic carrier bag, all over your: groceries (*); newly-done school art homework (**); non-washable, new designer jumper (***).

3. The large range of hosiery on display confused you so much that, instead of the tights you wanted, you have three packs of pop-socks or stockings (**).

4. The gloves you bought (on a freezing day) are clamped together with plastic thread – and you've no scissors with you (*).

IN THE SHOPS AND BOUTIQUES:

1. The changing-room is communal, so *everyone* can see you've picked a size too small (**).

2. They'll only let you take three things in to try at once – but you want four (**).

3. All the mirrors are so horribly lit that you can see every blemish, and look as though you've been dead six weeks (*).

4. You buy a really unusual necklace for £5 in the first shop – later you find they're all over town at £3 each. (**).

5. The security tag leaves a big hole in the fabric of your new dress when it's pulled out (*); or the assistant forgets to remove the tag, and you're arrested for shop-lifting as you go out through the door (***).

6. A sales assistant pounces on you as soon as you enter the shop, so you can't have a nose around (*); you're in a hurry, and can't find anything (***).

SCORE

Score:
Under 10 stars: **Not bad – you must be a talented shopper. A nice cup of tea and a couple of hours of junk TV, with your feet up, should put you right.**

10-20 stars: **Try a little quiet meditation, count to ten before doing anything drastic. Why not stick to the local shops next time? Or at least plan things better!**

More than 20 stars: **Come out from under the bed, and unclench your knuckles... that's better. Thump a cushion. Lie down with a damp cloth on your head – and buy a catalogue, next time!**

33

Secrets of a

A GUY'S EYE V

Ever wondered what's going through the mind of that local superstud as he locks you in a lip-numbing embrace? Now's the time to discover the shocking truth, naughty bits and all, about what that sexy bombshell is really feeling ... and we don't mean your left knee!

If you've got it, use it. That's what my big brother used to say to me. Sex appeal, I'm talking about. The kind of stuff that makes girls go gooey at a glance. Well, I can't help it if I look a dead ringer for George Michael, can I?

I've got them thinking I'm his long lost twin brother – and Wham! bang, thank you, mam, I've more females fainting at my feet than I can handle. Literally! Trouble is, I'm blowing it. Puffing and blowing it, trying to keep up with the frisky little beasts. Yes, you out there with the roaming hands and pouting lips!

But how can a poor guy live up to your expectation of a superstud without leaving him with more bags under his eyes than love bites as trophies of slavish affection?

Have you no consideration for a man's health?

Even my P.E. teacher told me to stop over-doing it when I flagged after five minutes as centre forward. Must have guessed what a hard night I'd had with Tracey the evening before. Can't keep her hands to herself for half a second, even when they're as sticky as a soggy Mars bar where she's been rifling through her packet of popcorn. But I haven't the heart to tell her to cool it and slow down.

MY GUY SUPERSTUD

I'd blow my image, and leave her and all my other admirers right in the lurch. They wouldn't know what to do with themselves, would they?

CHAT UP CHEATS

● **"I'd never dare chat up a real good looker. He'd think I was a real slag!"** ***Tracey, 15.***

It all starts before you even get to date them. They've got it all set in their minds. *He's* the one who's got to make the first move, give the lusty glances. Yes me! When it's all I can do to keep my eyes open after keeping up to Chrissie's kissing schedule the night before.

Coy looks are the most I get in the way of first moves. And all when I'd rather spend a night chatting to my mates, or even slumped in front of the telly.

But I've my reputation to keep up, so after a few once-overs I have to get into my chat up routine. I don't like to cause disappointment, y'see, I'm thoughtful like that.

CUT OUT THE KISSING

● **"Sexy looking guys don't want girls for friendship only. You can only be just good friends with grotty looking boys ..."** ***Julie, 16.***

Trouble is, I don't always want to date a girl just because I chat to her. Some guys, even with a reputation like mine, would love the opportunity, no – not to get a busty blonde for a bout of mud wrestling in a lonesome field, but to just be friends with a girl.

But how does a guy get a break like that? Search me. **THEY** think that all I want to do is love and lust after them, so every time I find a girl who'd make a great mate she takes it wrong and thinks I fancy her! And bang goes my chance of a friendship where we can have a bit of giggle and leave the love talk and steamy snogging sessions right out.

But try getting a girl to believe that "platonic" isn't something ageing whales eat to pep themselves up but a great way to enjoy being with another guy and you're asking for a flood out with the waterworks. It's love or bust ... and sometimes I don't want either!

FIRST NIGHT NERVES

● **"A guy with the reputation of a right Romeo makes me dead nervous. But then he's had so much experience I leave the talking to him in case I say something daft!"** ***Susie, 15.***

Blasé and cool, never a twitching nerve on display, That's the way I'm supposed to play it. But sometimes I feel on edge too! SHE thinks it's me who should set up the date, say where we're going, and crank up

YOUR GREAT

What Boys Have Never Dared Say Before.

TOO FAST

"Girls always blame boys for being too fast, but most girls I've dated are just as keen to get kissing as me – if not keener. I think it makes them feel better saying it's the guys who have pushed them into it ... as if there's something wrong in enjoying it."

Steven, 18.

SUSPICIOUS!

"It's guys who have the reputation of doing the dirty, but most girls I know are dead sneaky when it comes to two-timing!"

Trev, 17.

KISSING CRAZY

"If you date a girl and don't try and kiss her that first night she's likely to think there's something funny about you. But why should guys force it if they're not sure how they feel!"

Dave, 16.

Superstud

IEW OF YOU!

the conversation.

There I am, with a girl who's too nervous to utter more than a few blushing grunts when my stomach's sometimes so knotted with butterflies I feel they'll all fly out if I so much as open my mouth.

Then she starts thinking I'm throwing a moody, or coming on like some kind of superstar (well, I said I looked just like George Michael, didn't I?).

'Course if she's somehow got the idea that I'm some kind of flashman then she thinks I've a wallet as thick as an elephant's back thigh, so she doesn't so much as pretend to russle round in her bag when it comes to coughing up some cash to get into the disco, movies or doughnut store.

Maybe she's cracked enough to think I'd be offended if she offered to go Dutch. Offended! I'd grab it with two hands, and the money too!

ONLY AFTER ONE THING!

● **"Guys are only after one thing really. They spend their whole time seeing how far you'll go!"**
Chrissie, 16.

My mum said never more than one kiss on the first date, and that's what I used to try to stick to.

But most girls won't stand for that! It's not that they don't want too... they can't wait for more. They go on and on saying that it's the guys who are only after one thing, but who are they kidding? Fast? It's a wonder guys like me come out from some of their kisses without an added kiss of life to get the wind back into those plundered lungs!

And then I expect they go blaming me when they get in and their dad gives them a rocketing for being late – not to mention the quizzing over the ruffled hair, smudged make-up and rucked-up T-shirts. You want to see the state of my hair when they've finished with me! I get through a jar of hair gel a week!

What if I gave them a quick peck and ran for it? I'd be the town's laughing stock, that's what. The word would be round quicker than greased lightning ... "There's something funny about that Dave Brown. Good looks and clever comments. But he's all talk, and no action!" they'd twitter.

SOFA LOAFER

● **"Any good looking guy spends half his time checking to see which nights your parents are out. And those are the ones he wants to spend in!"** *Carrie, 16.*

Aha, another version on the theory that nice girls don't but all boys do. Try it on and see if they can qualify for an X certificate on the steamy scenes stakes, I mean.

Just as soon as Mum and Dad are out of the house they're suggesting a cosy night in, complete with your favourite video as added incentive.

Not that I ever see much of that. I might put my arm round her just to get comfy, and were off! That's her cue that our evening of lust has started, and there's no getting out of it – not even to see the best bits of the movie.

Okay, I'm not saying it's torture, but there are times when a guy wants to relax. But when he gets whipped up into a lather of frenzy by some busty brunnette, and egged on like he's going to win a gold medal what can she expect than for him to go for it.

Then she goes and says the party's over just when she's got him worked up a treat, and wonders why he finds it hard to switch off so quick. And she has the cheek to make out that she's the goody goody for stopping, and you're the dirty lust-master who needs keeping under control!

STOP BEING SEXIST

Now you've heard it with your own ears – the view of you from a superstud's point of view. Okay, so maybe you can take some of it with a pinch of salt – but you've got to admit that guys can become victims of stereotyping. If most guys walk round with preconceived ideas about girls then they get their fair share of sexist comments and thoughts chucked back in their direction too. Stop the rot by:

* Giving your guy a chance to show his true feelings, and not the ones he thinks you expect.
* Not boasting to your mates about how much he fancies you, and shows it! You'll give him a high reputation to live up to.
* Not always waiting for him to make the first move, Just because he looks good and acts cool doesn't mean he's confident.
* Stop kidding yourself that it's only him who wants to take the kissing and cuddling further and further. If you lead him on then don't blame him and label him a randy lad when you decide to stop and he doesn't get the message.
* Try not to see guys as boyfriends only. It's nice to have boys as friends as well as lovers, and enjoyable for them too!

EXPECTATIONS

SEX MAD!

"Girls think guys spend half their lives boasting about their sex lives. But have you ever heard a bunch of girls boast about what they've been up to the night before?!"
Jamie, 18.

And What YOU Said ...!

RUBBISH

"Ah, it must be awful to be a good looking guy. All those nasty girls running after you, molesting you at so much as a glance. It's enough to make you weep, isn't it?"
Lyn, 15.

OWN UP!

"Maybe some guys do feel they've been stereotyped, but it's just as hard for girls to break out of their stereotype. I could just imagine the look on the faces of guys if I asked them if they fancied a walk in the park!"
Susie, 16.

MY GUY COMPLETE PHOTO STORY

WHEN IT CAME TO LOVE–JULIA AND IAN WERE IN A DIFFERENT CLASS

Julia was shamed by her guy, so she kept him...

BEHIND CLOSED DOORS

Dates with Julia were never easy.
I DON'T UNDERSTAND IT. JULIA PROMISED ME SHE'D BE HERE BY SEVEN AND SHE'S ALREADY HALF AN HOUR LATE.
PSST!
Julia wanted their relationship to be secret.
JULIA? I DON'T BELIEVE IT. IS THAT YOU?
OF COURSE IT'S ME. WHO DID YOU THINK IT WAS?
I'M SORRY. I DIDN'T RECOGNISE YOU WITH THOSE GLASSES. ARE WE GOING TO A FANCY DRESS OR SOMETHING?
NO. I JUST DON'T WANT ANYBODY TO RECOGNISE ME. YOU KNOW HOW PEOPLE LIKE TO TALK. WHY DON'T WE GO TO THE PARK?
A few minutes later. . .
HOW LONG HAVE WE BEEN GOING OUT WITH EACH OTHER NOW, JULIA?
THREE WEEKS.
EXACTLY. DON'T YOU THINK IT'S ABOUT TIME PEOPLE KNEW? ARE YOU ASHAMED OF ME BECAUSE I WORK IN THE GARAGE?
WHY DO YOU HAVE TO TAKE EVERYTHING SO PERSONALLY?
WITH THE WAY YOU'RE CARRYING ON I'M NOT EVEN SURE YOU STILL WANT TO GO OUT WITH ME.
DON'T BE SILLY, IAN. OF COURSE I DO. IT WON'T BE LIKE THIS FOREVER.
SORRY I'VE GOT TO GO NOW, IAN. I'LL CALL YOU TOMORROW. DO YOU PROMISE YOU WON'T TELL ANYBODY THEN?
IF IT MAKES YOU FEEL BETTER.
Ian wouldn't tell anyone. . .
. . .except his best friend, Jerry.
WHAT? AND YOU JUST SAT THERE AND SAID YES?
WHAT ELSE COULD I DO? TRY AND PUT YOURSELF IN MY SHOES. I SUPPOSE SHE'S A BIT SHY ABOUT THESE THINGS. LOTS OF GIRLS ARE LIKE THAT.

COMPLETE PHOTO STORY

WELL, THAT'S WHAT I SAID. HE'S FAR TOO COMMON FOR SOMEONE LIKE YOU. ANYWAY, IT'S JUST STUPID GOSSIP, I SUPPOSE.
OF COURSE IT IS.
WELL, I MUST BE OFF THEN. I DO HOPE YOU'LL COME TO MY PARTY ON SATURDAY. YOU CAN EVEN BRING A FRIEND ALONG IF YOU LIKE. AS LONG AS THEY LOOK RESPECTABLE.
DON'T WORRY, YOU CAN TRUST ME.
BYE THEN.
But as soon as she'd closed the door the bell rang again.
REBECCA MUST HAVE FORGOTTEN SOMETHING.
But it was somebody else. . .
IAN! WHAT ARE YOU DOING HERE? HAVE YOU GONE OUT OF YOUR MIND?
OH, SORRY. IT'S JUST A LITTLE SURPRISE, THAT'S ALL.
DID ANYBODY SEE YOU COMING HERE?
WELL, APART FROM YOUR NEXT DOOR NEIGHBOUR'S CAT. . .
IT ISN'T SOMETHING TO JOKE ABOUT, IAN.
I'M NOT SURE I CAN TAKE THIS TREATMENT FOR MUCH LONGER, JULIA.
I KNOW IT ISN'T VERY NICE FOR YOU.
YOU'VE JUST GOT TO BE PATIENT, THAT'S ALL. JUST GIVE IT A WEEK AND I PROMISE WE WON'T HAVE TO PRETEND ANY MORE.
THAT'S WHAT YOU SAID LAST WEEK. JERRY RECKONS YOU'RE AFRAID YOUR SNOOTY FRIENDS MIGHT NOT APPROVE OF ME.
THAT'S NOT TRUE AT ALL. YOU DON'T BELIEVE HIM, DO YOU?
I DON'T KNOW, SOMETIMES I WONDER.
On Saturday morning . . .
HI? WHAT'S WRONG WITH YOU? YOU LOOK LIKE YOU'VE GOT A TOUCH OF THE BLUES. DON'T TELL ME YOUNG PRINCESS DI HAS BEEN GIVING YOU TROUBLE AGAIN?
NOT REALLY, IT'S NOT HER FAULT.

COMPLETE PHOTO STORY

"You know how people like to talk..."

MY GUY TESTS YOU OUT!

SECTION ONE

a) Name the lead singer with Spandau Ballet (they won't all be as easy as this, either, dears).
b) By which name is Gordon Sumner better known?
c) Where did Frankie Goes To Hollywood get their name from?
d) What was the title of Culture Club's first Number One hit?
e) From which group did Nick Heyward split in order to pursue a solo career?
f) Name the first box office hit film in which Prince played a starring role.
g) Who plays bass with Duran Duran?
h) Which famous person married Sean Penn?
i) Which band do brothers Martin and Gary Kemp play in?
j) From which country do Queen originate?

SECTION TWO

a) Name the lead singer with Level 42.
b) By which name is Fish better known?
c) Where did UB40 get their name from?
d) What was the title of Tears For Fears first Number One hit?
e) From which group did David Grant split in order to pursue a solo career?
f) Name the first box office hit film in which Madonna played a starring role.
g) Who plays bass with Frankie Goes To Hollywood?
h) Which famous person married Chrissie Hynde?
i) Which band do brothers Robin and Ali Campbell play in?
j) From which country do Aha originate?

SECTION THREE

a) Name the lead singer with Talking Heads
b) By which name is Norman Giscombe better known?
c) Where did Depeche Mode get their name from?
d) What was the title of Midge Ure's first Number One hit?
e) From which group did Stephen Duffy split in order to pursue a solo career?
f) Name the first box office hit film in which Bob Geldof played a starring role.
g) Who plays bass with Culture Club?
h) Which famous person married Giovana Cantone?
i) Which band do sisters Denise and Doris Stedman play in?
j) From which country do Mai Tai originate?

Think you could give the pop experts a run for their money? Make Paul Gambaccini and Co. quake in their all too big boots?

We'll, aha... (no, not the group) you haven't reckoned with us – possibly the most (ill?) informed little beasties you'll ever come across. *We* know John Taylor's inside trouser leg measurement; *we* know what Paul King likes nothing better than; *we* know everything and anything when it comes to the trivial and the not so trivial. Do you? We doubt it, but here's your chance to pit your wits against the very best... us (aren't we modest?).

ANSWERS

The earth shattering answers you're all waiting for with baited breath.

SECTION ONE a) Tony Hadley. b) Sting. c) From a billboard advertising a Frank Sinatra tour. d) Do You Really Want to Hurt Me? e) Haircut 100. f) Purple Rain. g) John Taylor. h) Madonna. i) Spandau Ballet. j) Britain.

SECTION TWO a) Mark King. b) Derek Dick from Marillion (and yes, we ARE serious). c) From the Social Security card number given to people out of work. d) Everybody Wants To Rule The World. e) Lynx. f) Desperately Seeking Susan. g) Mark O'Toole. h) Jim Kerr. i) UB40. j) Norway.

SECTION THREE a) David Byrne. b) Junior. c) From a Paris fashion shop. d) Forever And Ever (a 1976 hit when he was a member of the ultimate in screamibop bands, Slik). e) Duran Duran. f) Pink Floyd's The Wall. g) Roy Hay. h) Duran's Roger Taylor. i) Five Star. j) Holland.

Well, how did you fare? – honest answers, please. If you scored:

0 – 10 Don't know why you bothered attempting the quiz, really. You *must* have known what a pin head you'd make of yourself! Or are you so swathed in self-conceit that you really thought you knew all the answers?

May we suggest that you either: a) treat yourself to a generous supply of pop mags and total immersement in what we call popular radio – not Radio Four's Gardening Hour, or; b) sincerely hope that no one else gets to see this feeble attempt at musical knowledge – tear these pages out and stuff them under the bed immediately.

11 – 20 Hmmm, not bad for a complete and utter beginner. But we bet your kid sister who's still into mwaking the pwetty things out of washing up bwottles on Blue Peter did mounds better than you. *And* we bet she had her hands tied behind her back and her eyes closed at the time.

Study hard though, and you'll be ready to face the world by about... ooh, the year 2054.

21 – 30 Don't call us, we'll call you (or rather we won't, otherwise you could just be after our jobs). Are you sure you didn't cheat just the inciest little bit? No? In that case, may we doff our caps to you, oh great one, and suggest that in future you refrain from being such a nauseating little show-off, okay?

QUIZ

MY GUY LOVE STORY

A group from school are about to leave for the annual trip to Germany. A crowd of us stand in front of the science block and watch the lucky ones load their luggage on the coach. They are wearing their new summer gear: baggy pink dungarees, white jackets, little canvas boots in pastel colours. Like a lot of well-fed, exotic birds, they look, chattering excitedly, calling to each other: pinks and blues and bright, dazzling white. One in a flame-coloured catsuit: Lorraine.

JUST THE BEGINNING

The dull grey sparrows standing to one side are the ones who aren't going to Germany, me included. We are looking drab in school uniform but are smiling bravely, shrugging, pretending we aren't the slightest bit bothered.

Dave Marsh is one of the sparrows, standing next to me.

"Wish they'd hurry and go!" he says. "I mean, do we *have* to stand here while they show off all their new clothes and strut up and down preening themselves?"

"I think there's some hold up with Lorraine's luggage," I say. "It won't fit into the luggage compartment."

"Trust her – she's probably got a cabin trunk or something."

NATURAL

"Yeah, trust her," I echo, looking at her enviously. As well as the flame-coloured catsuit she's wearing a white plaited headband over which a few casual curls fall into her eyes. It looks so natural that I know she must have been up half the night doing it. She'll be the Princess Di of the holiday: clothes for every occasion and never the same thing twice.

"It'll be quiet around here for the next couple of weeks without them all," Dave says sadly.

I nod, biting my lip. It'll be quiet all right – and as far as I'm concerned I'll be quite happy to hibernate until the coach comes back. Stuart is going, too, you see. He's the one with the electric blue canvas jacket and the thick, black hair slicked back at the sides and spikey on top so that he looks like a bird of paradise.

I like him a lot and I think he likes me – but I'm not really going out with him. Lorraine is the same – not really going out with him either, and that's what I'm worried about. He treats us both the same, you see, dances with us both at discos, chats to us, buys us drinks, but that's as far as it goes. Rumour has it (who starts these rumours?) that he's going to make a decision this month, now that the exams are over, about who he's going to ask out.

If only I could have got to go to Germany with the school. I think it might have been me. Dad's out of work, though, so I didn't even ask. As it is now, I think Lorraine will win hands down. Well, they're going to be together a lot, aren't they? All that walking in the Black Forest business and swimming in lakes with waterfalls and going up two-by-two in the chair lifts . . . it can't fail. It's obvious that when they come back they're going to be a pair.

"Lorraine looks tanned already," Dave says, still next to me.

I give a short laugh. "She's got a sun bed at home, you can see *that*. I mean, you can't tell me that it's natural – no more natural than the hair streaks!"

JEALOUSY

Dave grins. "Do I detect a trace of jealousy in your voice?"

"Too right!" I say. "How is it some people have all the luck: the sun beds and the clothes and the money?"

"You wanted to go on the Germany trip, did you?"

"Of course I did! Didn't everyone? Didn't you?"

He shakes his head. "Not really. I quite fancy going abroad but I'm a terrible traveller. I'd feel bad before the coach got to the end of the road."

I'm just looking at Dave, thinking that he's quite nice and it's funny that I've never spent much time talking to him before, when my attention is distracted by Mr. Wilkinson, one of the teachers who're going, running up and trying to do a head count.

"Listen, everyone, this is important! Can you keep still a moment – and stop all the shouting!" he says, but they're all mucking around too much to hear him.

"Looks like it's going to be hot at the weekend," Dave says, looking up at the sky. "A real scorcher."

"Sunny here isn't the same as sunny abroad," I say wistfully. "It just gets hot and stuffy here, so you can't breathe. *They'll* be swimming in lakes and windsurfing and all that."

"The old swimming baths will be open – you know, the open air one. It should be OK there."

"Mmm," I say, hardly listening. I'm watching Lorraine; she's talking in a cute way to Stuart with her head on one side.

"Honestly, Stu, I'm terrified of heights! If we go on one of those chair lifts you've got to promise you'll stay with me."

SICK

Stuart laughs and says something to her I can't quite hear. I feel quite sick and I'm not even on the coach.

"Everyone aboard!" Mr. Wilkinson says, giving up the idea of a roll-call, and there's a great surge as everyone bundles forward. I look at Stuart for the last time for two whole weeks.

"You're very quiet," Dave says. "I expect it's... I mean, I don't suppose you're too pleased about Stuart going off for two weeks and Lorraine being there."

I shake my head. "No, I'm not very pleased," I say. Talk about the understatement of the year.

"I'm never sure about you and Stuart – whether you're going out with him or not."

"That makes two of us," I say with a faint smile.

They all settle down in the coach. Lorraine is at a window seat and Stuart is next to her. She's offering him something from a bag; they are very close.

The coach starts up and I sigh and go to turn away but Dave stops me. "Don't let them see you miserable," he says. "Wave – leave 'em laughing!'

Everyone starts to shout and yell their goodbyes and I do, too. Stuart sees me, grins and waves in an absent-minded way, as if he can't quite remember who I am. The coach moves off, we stand waving until our arms ache. I smile until I can't see the coach any more and then the smile drops away from me and I slump.

GIGGLE

"Now," Dave says, "you're not to crumble to bits, you're not to sit and brood for two weeks!"

"OK, doc," I say.

"For a start, how about coming swimming with me? I know the local baths aren't exactly wonderful..."

"Burnham Pool!" I say. "It's all chipped tiles and grass cuttings floating on the water!"

"And changing rooms with no doors and treble chlorine in the water to make your eyes sting!"

I begin to giggle in spite of myself. "Let me get this straight," I say, "all the others are going off to swim in crystal clear lakes and jump about under waterfalls and you're offering me red eyes and a lot of grass cuttings in my hair?"

He takes my hand. "Well, it'll be something to do. A start."

I smile at him. I don't feel so much like a neglected sparrow now.

"Why not?" I say. "I've got nothing to lose."

An end and a beginning on the same day?

Well, maybe...

THE END

The POW

LOVE

There's nothing like the power of love to take over our lives, control them, even make or break them. It's one of the strongest emotions there is and no matter how hard we try, we just can't fight it. People constantly try though, as its power isn't always positive. Sometimes love can make us do things we live to regret for ever. So read on and discover what it did for these readers....

JEALOUSY

Mary had always been jealous of her cousin, Sharon. Sharon seemed to have everything – good looks, a new job as a bank clerk, and as if that wasn't enough, she had Dave, the kind of guy Mary had always dreamt about.

"He was perfect in my eyes, "Mary confided." Tall, gentle, enough money to enjoy life, and a really good job. It just didn't seem fair that it was Sharon who found him."

And what made it worse was the pressure which Mary's Mum kept putting on her to find a boyfriend. "She was always holding Sharon up as someone who was better than me – I hated it, and somehow, Sharon's mere existance made me lack any confidence in myself to actually be able to relax with boys. I felt boring and useless, not good enough for anyone."

The more Mary got to know Dave, the more she liked him.

And soon, the only times she made any effort with her appearance was when he called round with Sharon.

"It was as though he was my boyfriend," Mary told us. "That he was coming just to see me."

And it only took Dave a couple of months to catch on.

"He seemed flattered," Mary went on, "and started flirting with me, whenever Sharon's back was turned. Sharon, of course, didn't notice. She was so confident of Dave she'd never dream if he could be in any way disloyal."

Then, one evening, Dave slipped Mary a note arranging a date for the following night.

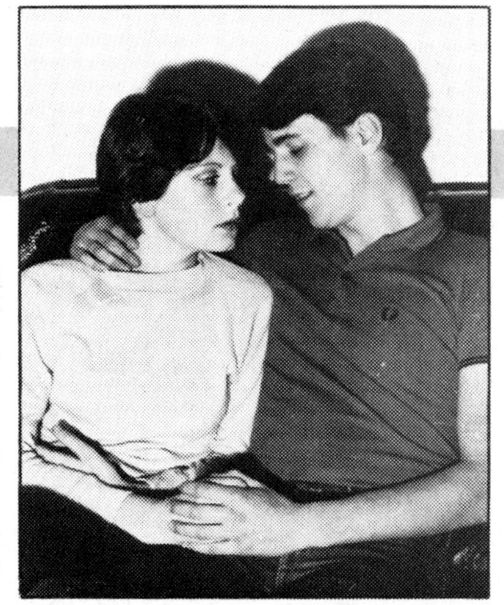

LONG DISTANCE LOVE

"As soon as I saw Pete, I felt he was someone I'd always be with. It seemed so right."

Linda was on holiday with her parents when she met Pete.

They disliked him on the spot – she was seeing someone back home in Aberdeen whom they liked and secretly hoped she'd marry.

Pete and Linda spent every day possible together, under the disapproving eyes of her parents.

And, behind Linda's back, they decided to leave a day earlier than arranged.

"When I woke up in the morning, Mum and Dad were frantically packing their suitcases. They didn't even give me time to ring Pete, to explain."

A tearful Linda got in the car with her parents as they set off on the long trip home.

"After a few hours, we stopped at a motorway service station. I wouldn't get out of the car.

"Suddenly, I noticed Mum's purse in the dashboard. I knew it would hold at least £50. So I picked it up, and got out of the car.

"I managed to hitch a lift to a few miles of Pete's house, then called him. He'd been frantic.

"I just threw myself in his arms and cried my heart out."

As soon as Linda's parents knew she was missing they called the police and it wasn't long before they arrived at Pete's doorstep.

"It was hell, and I was more or less kept a prisoner until I got home."

"It was only a few months 'til my sixteenth birthday – it's legal in Scotland to leave home then and on that day, I got the first train down to Pete. We've been together and are hoping to get married. My parents? They just don't want to know. But my love for Pete has made all the heartbreak worth-while."

ER of

"I couldn't believe it," said Mary. "It was like a dream come true." He took me to a really smart club in town and was so attentive.

"Then, on the way home, he stopped the car near an area of woodland where lots of couples go.

"I was thrilled at the thought of a quick kiss and cuddle, but he had other ideas.

"He reckoned I'd led him on to make him think I'd sleep with him.

"It was awful, and once I'd convinced him that I didn't have any intention of sleeping with him, he drove me home in sullen silence."

Next day, Mary felt so hurt and betrayed by Dave, she just couldn't think straight.

"All my feelings against Sharon just spilled over and I found myself blurting out to Mum what had happened."

Mary's mum told Sharon and soon it was all out in the open.

"Sharon chucked Dave then, and she hasn't spoken to me since.

"Now, I can't bear to even think about it all. But I can still remember the power of that love I felt for him – it was evil."

THREE'S A CROWD

"It had always been Tony, Mike and me – ever since we were at school together," Kath began.

"We were just friends, nothing else. Or so we thought until Tony's job took him away to London for six months.

"At first Mike and I carried on as before, mucking around, acting like kids. Then, on my birthday, he took me out for a really special meal. He looked nervous about being with me, which was weird considering how long we'd known each other.

"Then out of the blue, he blurted out that he wanted a lot more than friendship.

"I was shocked at first, then, after a few minutes realised that maybe friendship had grown into love for both of us. I couldn't wait to tell Mum. She'd always liked Mike and used to tease me about him when I was little.

"So we started going out together properly, at first, forgetting about Tony in London."

Mike got a letter a few months after he and Kath had started going out, saying that Tony would be arriving at the weekend.

"At first, I was thrilled to bits, really looking forward to telling him our news. Then panic set in. It had all changed. We weren't just three kids any more. It was me and Mike, together, and Tony on the sidelines.

"He hit the roof when he found out, and spent the whole weekend at home. Then, on the Sunday night he came round to see me.

"He was all white and shaking and started telling me he only went to London to earn enough money to be able to ask me out, even get engaged. Then he went on about how nasty Mike was to girls and had been two-timing me all along.

"Then he rushed out, talking about the way we'd deceived him.

"Later, Mike rang to say Tony had been to see him and said I was two-timing."

Luckily, Mike and Kath realised exactly what Tony was trying to do.

"His love was for both of us, for our friendship," Kath said. "He just didn't want our happy threesome to change. We haven't seen him since, and we're both pretty sad at what happened. But at least we have our own love now – and he could have been part of that."

MYGUY CONFESSIONS

FAT GIRLS CAN'T HAVE FUN...

Jan was tired of being fat and cuddly...

I didn't have a lot of time. I raced upstairs, reached under the bed for one bar of chocolate, changed my mind and grabbed two, and then tore at the outside wrappings of the first one, and pushed it into my mouth.

"Janine!" my sister's voice called from the hallway. "Are you up there? I'm coming up!"

"Janine!" she called, outside my door. I pushed the paper into my top drawer. No one had to know. Later I'd flush it down the toilet.

"Hey, long time no see! I brought the bridesmaid's dress..." Cathy beamed, throwing open the door. Then she stopped dead in her tracks.

"Jan...?" she murmured, bewildered. "I just don't believe it... This dress'll never fit you! Mum told me that you'd lost weight but..."

My reflection bounced back at me from the mirror. Lost weight? If only! But the gross ugly kid mirrored there was the same huge horror she'd always been. Maybe just a little slimmed down. Perhaps. But still a hamster. Isn't that what Cathy's fiancé, Paul, had called me, that night he'd come round to meet me, and talk to Mum and Dad about the wedding?

I'd have died for that guy. He was tall and hunky, unbelievably good-looking. He was a pharmacist in the hospital where my sister was doing her nursing training, down in London, but he could've passed for an actor or a pop star any day.

And that night Cathy, glowing slimline Cathy, as successful and perfect as ever, had said.

"You can be our bridesmaid, Janine."

And Paul had ruffled my mousey hair and grinned.

"OK, hamster?"

Hamster. Piglet. Spare Tyre. I'd heard them all, at one time or another. So I started my diet.

It was a pretty complicated thing that I worked out for myself. It involved counting calories, weighing everything that I ate, weighing myself three times a day, keeping charts all the time.

SKINNY

"Jan, what is it?" Cathy asked, walking towards me with the peach satin dress over her arm. She laid it carefully on my bedroom chair and put her hands on my shoulders. "You're so skinny and sick-looking. Are you ill? Have you seen a doctor?"

"Who needs a doctor when there's a nurse in the family, even if she *is* away from home most of the time!" I snapped. "Is Paul with you?"

"Not this time. I just came up to try the bridesmaid's dress on you. I have to go back tonight. But it was ready, and I had a day off and I couldn't wait, and...You'd better wash those hands before you try it on. What's that? Chocolate? Couldn't be, 'cos Mum says you've hardly eaten anything this last three months..."

"Er, I'll wash my hands, then," I stammered, pulling away from her grip, running to the bathroom.

I needed that excuse. Desperately. I'd been on pins, hoping I'd be able to get away before the stuff went into my stomach and started turning into fat. Already, I could feel it happening. My stomach churned with panic, churned and churned.

But I made it into the bathroom, locked the door, turned on both the taps, pushed my finger into my throat, and got rid of it. One more sin that wouldn't harm me again. I heaved repeatedly, until I was sure there was no more chocolate contaminating my insides. Then I stepped on the scales.

There was a banging at the bathroom door.

"Open this door!" Cathy yelled.

Smiling, confident, I did just that. The scales had just told me I still weighed a little under six stone. I was winning.

Cathy sniffed, then turned the taps off, and grabbed my hands. They were still streaked with chocolate. She said nothing, just looked from my hands into my eyes.

"You've got a problem," she said, very softly. "Want to talk about it?"

"Nothing to talk about. I don't know what you mean!" I said, hotly.

"Jan, weight loss like this, the high colour in your cheeks, the skeletal look you've got, could suggest a serious illness..."

I laughed.

"These were under your pillow, too. Laxatives. What do you need laxatives for? It all adds up to a classic case of anorexia!"

"Huh!" I screamed at her. "Think you know everything, don't you? Think you've got everything and everyone at your feet, just because you're slim and pretty! And Paul, you've got him, too."

TEARS

I broke down into screaming sobs. Cathy's arms folded round me, and her warm tears trickled down my neck.

"Oh Jan!" she murmured, "you're lovely as you were, warm and shy and affectionate and intelligent. We all love you so much. Don't you know that? Don't you realise?"

I didn't. But if love is expressed by the care and attention I got in hospital, by Cathy's total concern and endless visits, by Paul's hugs, by Mum's tears, perhaps I realise now. Perhaps I'm getting better. Perhaps people can love me, just for my inadequate self. And perhaps I can try to like me, too.

THE CASEBOOK 14th Oct 1986

NAME: **JAN CARTER** AGE: **16** HOME: **HULL**

WHAM!
MY GUY

Clear the way for a spotless complexion and go soft on our face-saving skincare guide.

bRAVE

If you want good skin you've got to work at it, and that means careful cleansing, toning and moisturising morning and night, plus a healthy diet of food, rest and play. Caring for your skin will not only bring rewards now, but in later years too.

SWITCHED ON

First find out your skin type and then get to work with the right skincare programme.

OILY skin looks and feels greasy, and is often accompanied by spots, pimples, open pores, blackheads or acne. It's caused by overactive sebaceous glands producing too much sebum (oil) as a result of changes in hormone levels, which is why oily and spotty skins are so common during teenage years.

The one good point about oily complexions is that sebum is the skin's layer of protection against moisture loss, so an extra dose means your skin is less prone to wrinkles.

DRY skin feels taut and may be flaky. It's also often sensitive and prone to broken veins, spidery red lines on the cheeks. This condition is caused by a lack of sebum, so the skin isn't adequately protected against moisture loss.

COMBINATION skin is a combination of dryness on the cheeks, sides of the forehead and throat, plus an oily skin type in the T zone – the centre of your forehead, down the nose and onto the chin. So, use different cleansers on each area, a mild toner all over, and a creamy moisturiser on the dry patches.

SENSITIVE skin is easily irritated and will become red in patches or all over. Treat with a hypo-allergenic range which contains no perfume or irritants.

CLEAN IT UP

Cleansing is the first step in your skincare routine and there are lots of products to help you clean up your act. Choose from creams, creamy liquids, milks, gels, cleansing bars and foaming washes – one designed for your skin type – and decide whether you prefer the wipe-off or wash-off variety.

If you don't feel clean until you've washed your face, use a cleansing bar or foaming wash, made specially for use on the face. Never use normal household soap as it will upset the balance of your skin. Massage soap onto your face and neck, and then rinse with warm water and pat dry. If your skin feels taut and dry afterwards, then it's possible you're not rinsing the soap off properly. Don't use a flannel, especially if you've got spots, as it will spread infection.

If using a creamy cleanser, gently massage the cream into your skin and then wipe it off with cotton wool or a soft

NEW FACE

tissue moistened with warm water. This will help remove the cleanser thoroughly and won't drag your skin.

A milky cleanser, on the other hand, should be applied straight to moistened cotton wool and gently wiped over the face and neck.

Whatever you choose, always work from the neck upwards, being careful not to drag your skin, particularly the delicate tissue around your eyes.

GET FRESH

Remove any last traces of grease the cleanser may have left, and freshen up with a toner. But ignore claims that they'll close up pores, they won't.

Generally you'll find that fresheners suit dry and normal skin types, toners are best for greasy skins, and astringents should be used only on very greasy and problem skins.

Or why not save some money and make your own toner? If you've dry, normal, sensitive, or combination skin, decant some mineral water into a small plant spray and give your face a refreshing squirt.

Or go into your chemist and get some rose-water or orange flower water. These can be used by themselves or again mixed with mineral water and poured into a plant spray for a soft, fresh mist.

For a slightly more astringent effect, mix rose-water with witch hazel, again available from your chemist – just ask at the counter. For oily skins, mix equal quantities of witch hazel and rose-water, and for normal skins try two parts rose-water with one part witch hazel, and gently wipe over your skin with cotton wool.

SOFT TOUCH

Keep skin soft and smooth by moisturising after cleansing and toning. Moisturisers act not as their name suggests by putting moisture into the skin but imitate sebum, the skin's natural way of keeping the skin soft and supple. Both sebum and man-made moisturisers guard against excessive moisture loss.

Greasy and normal skins need a thin, light lotion which is quickly absorbed into the top, dead layer of skin, whereas dry skins need a heavier cream.

For effective moisturising, dampen the skin first, as the top, dead layer of skin will absorb a small amount of this water. Then gently massage your moisturiser into the skin, working from the neck upwards, trapping in the water layer for extra protection. Again, when applying moisturisers be careful not to drag your skin, particularly the delicate tissue around your eyes.

Keep following steps 1, 2 and 3, and you'll soon see the benefits. When you're older, you'll be glad you cared for your skin now!

CUT TO FIT

Knowing what suits you is an important step in style. So, read on and dress to flatter.

The clotheshorses of fashion strutting along catwalks and posing in magazines are at least five foot, six inches and a 'perfect' size ten. They look wonderful in anything designers and fashion editors decide to dress them in. However, not all of us mere mortals match these statistics, so clever dressers should learn how to flatter their own figure type, as well as their personality, and be confident about their looks. Everyone has some complaint to make about their figures, even models, so learn to accept what you've got, play up on good points and play down those you're not so keen on.

BIG IS BEAUTIFUL

Larger figures slim down in dark and cold colours such as blue, green, purple, brown and greys. Pale and warm shades on the other hand are not for you.
Reds, yellow, orange, and yellow-based pinks and ginger tones enlarge the figure.
Go for loosely fitting, but not baggy separates, avoid the tent-like Demis Roussos look.
Choose separates which tone in with each other, avoiding a definite change in colour from top half to the lower half which draws attention to your waistline.
A loose, low-slung belt is a flattering way of hiding a bulging tummy.
Another good tip to remember is to wear a skirt, tights and shoes in the same colour, as it has a slimming effect.
Also wear long necklaces and bold eyecatching earrings.
The important thing to remember is not to try and hide yourself in boring low-key clothes.
For inspiration, take a look at the way Alison Moyet dresses, for instance. She's taken advantage of all the loose-fitting designer clothes around, and manages to look fashionable and eyecatching, with a confidence about the way she looks which makes her even more attractive.

SMALL TALK

Small girls are at their best in simple, clean-cut shapes, avoiding fuss and frills. If you fancy wearing patterns, then choose small ones, rather than large prints which will swamp you.
If you feel you're a bit too skinny, then fill out with bright colours, or pastels, whites and creams. And for longer-looking legs wear shoes and tights in the same colour.
Finally, keep accessories to the minimum. Simple but strong pieces of jewellery look best.

PART TIME

If you have wide hips, then avoid tops and jackets which stop at the curviest point of your hips. Draw attention to the area above your waistline by wearing eyecatching, large earrings, necklaces and brooches (although not necessarily all at the same time), padded shoulders and tops with interesting details. And if you've a small waist, emphasise it with a wide belt.
If you've a thick waist, disguise it by wearing loose tops over straight skirts and trousers, with a low-slung belt over the top.
Small busts can wear almost anything, but large busts will be emphasized by tight-fitting tops, whereas looser, draped tops over straight skirts and tapered trousers will make them less noticeable. So, take you pick.

CONFIDENCE

But remember, rather than complain about the parts you don't like, think about the good points, and gain confidence in your body. Who's to say that big hips aren't attractive anyway? Different things are attractive to different people. What is a perfect figure?

You...and your body!

The Inside Facts!

Understanding our bodies isn't easy when there's so much to figure out, especially through the teenage years. But follow our body guide and you'll have a lot more facts at your fingertips.

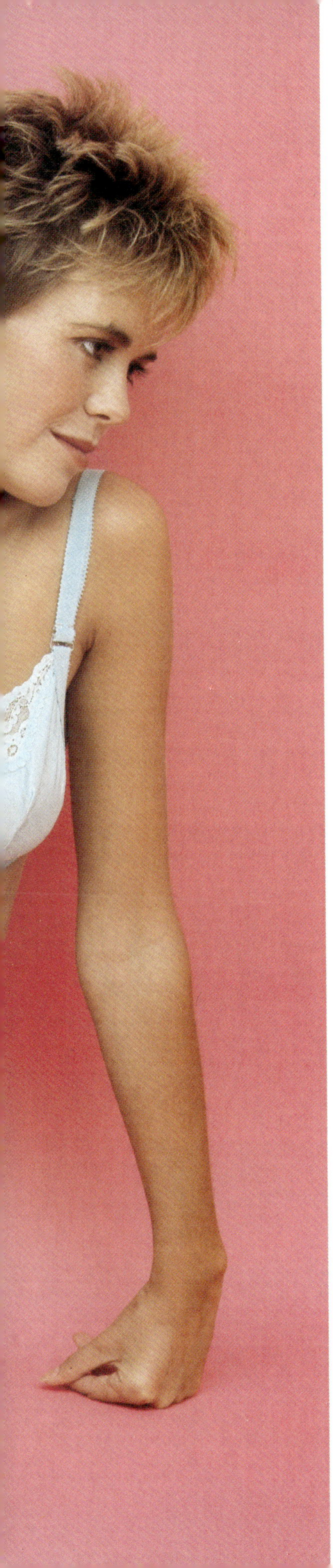

A is for acne which attacks most of us at some time. Severe acne must be treated by a doctor but a sensible diet and a scrupulous cleansing regime may help to control it.

B is for breasts. We all worry about their shape and size, but there is no average. So don't panic if yours look different – only expensive, unnecessary surgery can change the shape.

C stands for cystitis which all of us can suffer from. It's easily treated provided you get to a doctor early and take the whole course of antibiotics.

D is for dentist, whom you must see every six months. Keep teeth clean by brushing three times a day and lay off sweet foods.

E means energy, which you should have loads of. If not, examine your diet carefully to make sure you're eating enough vegetables, protein and vitamins.

F stands for fibre. It's not just a trendy word but a very necessary requirement for our digestive systems. Find it in vegetables, fruit and wholemeal products.

G is for glands which produce vital hormones, to keep the body functioning.

H is for our hair, which needs a good varied diet to stay healthy and strong.

I stands for injections. Most of you should, by now, have had the Rubella jab which protects against German Measles. This illness can cause damage to a foetus if the mother is pregnant.

J means junk food which can make you feel lethargic, cause spots and is worth avoiding. The odd hamburger shouldn't damage the body but a constant diet of them will result in a lack of necessary vitamins.

K is for kissing which, believe it or not, is very good for the body, so the experts say. So pucker up and enjoy it.

L is for legs which should be kept smooth and hair-free, either with regular waxing or depilatory creams. But before you use the creams, do a small skin test to ensure there's no allergy.

M is for menstruation. This happens every 28 days but can vary, as no two girls have the same cycle. For a comprehensive guide, check out *Have You Started Yet?* by Ruth Thomson, published by Piccalo.

N means nicotine which can cause cancer, chest complaints and bronchitis, so don't start smoking.

O is for ovaries, the female sex organs which produce eggs and are the first step in the cycle which leads to menstruation.

P is for the Pill which can be prescribed by a doctor or the Family Planning clinic. But you should only consider taking it if you're seriously involved in a long-term relationship.

Q stands for those questions you constantly want to ask. If your mum won't answer them, maybe you have a guidance teacher at school who will help.

R means rest. So no matter how often you fancy staying up to watch the late night movie, don't do it. Lack of sleep causes irritability, bad health and causes lack of concentration.

S is for slimming. You should never diet without first seeing your doctor for advice.

T stands for thrush, a fungus which grows in the vagina. The fungus can cause discharge which can be very itchy. See your doctor for help.

U means understanding – and that's everything from knowing about your own body to taking into account other people's feelings.

V means vitamins. With a healthy, balanced diet you shouldn't need them, but winter colds can often be kept at bay with Vitamin C. Vitamin B6 can help PMT – ask your doctor for info.

W is for warts, which, though harmless, can look unsightly. Compound W, carefully applied, can get rid of them, but often they disappear of their own accord. Genital warts need professional treatment.

X means exercise and that doesn't mean running for the bus in the morning. Try swimming, jogging or joining a badminton club.

Y stands for yoga, which is a perfect relaxation exercise, and it tones up the body.

Z is for zzzzz. No, we can't live without sleep so make sure you get eight hours a night.

HOWARD
JONES
MY GUY

SPANDAU BALLET
MY GUY

DURAN
DURAN
MY GUY

FRA

THE EAR

frankie Goes To Hollywood's meteoric rise to the heady heights of fame and fortune has been so well documented since 1984, that you'd have had to have been in a time-warp not to know about it. But what of those pre-fame days, when they were just five scousers existing down Liverpool way? Unearth a few facts about each one of them, and you'll soon see they had anything but *an easy life.*

CREDENTIALS

Holly – lead vocals. Born William Johnson, February 19, 1960. Has two brothers and one sister.
Paul – backing singer and dancing. Born Paul Steven Rutherford, December 8, 1959.
Ped – drums. Born Peter Gill, March 8, 1960.
Mark – bass. Born Mark William O'Toole, January 6, 1964.
Nasher – lead guitar. Born Brian Philip John Nash, May 20, 1963.

CHILDHOOD

Holly was born in Wavertree, Liverpool, just around the corner from Penny Lane.
Mark: "The earliest thing I can remember is from when I was six. I was playing in our old house and I ran smack into the couch and hit me chin. I bit my tongue off and had to go and get it sewn back on at the hospital."
Nasher's parents say of their sprog: "He was an unbelievably big baby, a good ten-pounder. We thought he'd be at least six foot six, because by the time he was two he was already three foot high."
Mark and **Nasher** are cousins – "We were always close," says Nash.
Mark: "My family's dead close. My sister still lives at home – I've got three brothers, two sisters, me mum, dad, and a nephew all living in the same house."
Holly: "When I was a kid I wanted to be a ventriloquist, then an archaeologist."
Mark: I used to like *The Champions* and *The Avengers. The Champions* were the ones who used to wear polo necks. They crashed in the Himalayas and they had super powers."
Nasher: *Magpie* was awful, but *Blue Peter's* John Noakes was brilliant. He had loads of bottle doing all these things that no one'll do any more like jumping out of planes and getting stuck on mountains in Scotland. He was a bit of a plank, like, but he was dead funny."
Ped: "I used to watch a lot of bands like The Who and Led Zeppelin on the television and wished I could be there."
Holly: I was a choirboy, but only because I liked dressing up. *Cassocks.* It was fab. I used to go on choir outings and you used to get sixpence a show. It was like being in the theatre."
Holly's father, **Eric:** "He didn't have a particularly good voice! Both his brothers John and Jim, and even his sister Clare, were much better singers."

PREVIOUS JOBS

Mark: "I only ever had one job, working as an apprentice carpenter for Liverpool Corporation. I did go for another, as a butcher's assistant, but I didn't get that."

NKIE:

LY DAYS

Ped used to be a wood machinist but he was made redundant.
Holly: "I was on the dole for ages but I did occasional work. I did some labouring in Wapping, converting warehouses into studios on Metropolitan Wharf. At one time I was living on £23.50 a week on the Social. Then, in 1979 the DHSS stopped my money. They wanted to send me off to Birmingham to take part in a rehabilitation course as a cuddly-toy maker or a gardener."
Nasher: "My apprenticeship started on simple things like fixing school fridges, mending the cookers in school kitchens, rewiring houses. After a year of that it was back to working on the bench as an electrician."

TEENAGE LIFE

Holly: "I started writing songs at 13 in our front room."
Eric Johnson: "Billy's interest in music started as a teenager. He bought himself an Anteus guitar for £4 when he was 13. A year later I bought him an acoustic Epiphone Jumbe from a fella for £59."
Holly: "Every teenager has a bad patch. The reaction at home to my lifestyle wasn't too hot. My dad used to think he had a walking freak show for a son."
Paul's sister **Monica:** "From the age of about 14 he was making clothes. I think it's something he could still do."
Nasher was thought to be a gifted mimic who specialised in John Cleese and Frankie Howerd. His interest in music started when he was given a series of guitars – best chum Mike Murphy donated one, the O'Tooles lent him another, and his parents bought him two.
Mark: "I remember when we used to go and sunbathe on Holly's roof – he had a top flat – and we used to write on the tiles, 'We will be famous one day' and the date. Wonder if they're still there?"

THE MAKING OF FRANKIE

The name **Frankie Goes To Hollywood** was taken from a Fifties' poster advertising a visit to Los Angeles by Frank Sinatra.
Holly and **Paul** first met in the back of a taxi on the way home from a Liverpool club.
Holly was introduced to **Mark, Ped** and **Nasher** in Virgin Records, where Mark was "trying to cop off with this girl in this clothes shop round the corner..."
Mark says of the incident: "When he was in **Big In Japan,** I used to think, 'God, he must be dead famous'. He wasn't really, though he was a bit eccentric. He helped me with this girl who worked in a shop. I fancied her but was too shy to go in and ask her out. Holly made me go in. And she turned me down!"
A couple of years later after 'loads of different permutations', they got together and formed **Frankie Goes To Hollywood.**
Paul: "Originally they played a couple of gigs without me. When I saw them for the first time I didn't know what was going on at all. It was just incredibly wild. So I jumped on stage and joined in. That's when it started for me. It was like my dream really, to be in a band like that."

SUCCESS

By the time of their first performance they had written just three songs – *Love's Got A Gun* (which became *Wish You Were Here*), the mega hit *Relax* and *Two Tribes.*
After a slot on *The Tube,* Trevor Horn rang them up and asked them to join his new record label, Zang Tuum Tumb.
When Mike Read banned debut release *Relax,* it immediately shot to Number One.
And the rest, as they say, is history.

ALL OVER YOU

Follow our top-to-toe beauty treatments and make sure you look good all over.

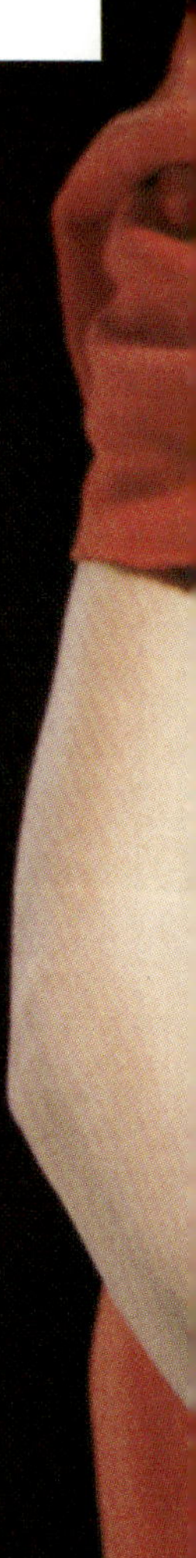

PURE & SIMPLE

Start from the top with a purifying and toning facial every six weeks.

First secure your hair away from your face and tie a towel around your top half. Then cleanse your face and run a bowlful of steaming water. Add to this a few fragrant herbs if you like, such as rosemary or peppermint. Drape a towel over your head and bend over the water letting the steam waft in your face.

But don't get too close or you'll come out looking like a beetroot. If your skin is oily, then steam it for 3-4 minutes, if it's dry 7-8 minutes. After a steaming, now's the time to treat spots and blackheads, as skin is soft and warm.

Dab a little antiseptic over the area under attack and then, with your fingertips covered in tissue, very gently squeeze spots where pus and blackheads are present. Don't squeeze hard red spots as they'll only get worse. Then dab again with antiseptic.

Now pluck your eyebrows as hairs come out more easily after steaming. Remove straggly hairs from underneath your brow.

Next, apply a face mask for your skin type, and place a couple of slices of cucumber on your eyelids to refresh them. Lie back and relax.

Finally, give skin a healthy glow with a massage. Dot moisturiser for your skin type over your face and neck, then starting from the base of your neck, massage with gentle circular movements. But be very careful not to drag your skin, especially around the eyes.

HEAVENLY BODIES

Our faces get pampered day and night, so isn't it about time we gave a bit more thought to the skin on the rest of our bodies, every time we take a bath?

Next time you're taking the plunge make sure it's into warm water rather than boiling hot. Hot water will dehydrate your skin. Then add a capful of bath oil, or baby oil (unless you've got greasy patches of skin). Don't lie back and soak for too long, instead get to work with a gentle soap and an invigorating rub down with a loofah. Lazing around in the water too long will dry out your skin. If you've got tiny raised bumps on the back of your arms, now's the time to massage them with an exfoliating cream or use natural sea salt for a cheap alternative. Then hop out and pat yourself dry. Massage in generous helpings of body lotion using firm circular movements of your palms.

HANDS UP

So you're going out, your make-up and hair are immaculate but are your hands looking a little worse for wear? If so, try giving them a manicure.

First file your nails into a gentle oval shape using the fine side of an emery board. Move the file in one direction only, from the side to the centre – not in a back and forth action as this will lead to rough edges – and round off the top.

Now soak your fingers for a couple of minutes in warm, soapy water. This will help remove dirt and soften the cuticle. Using an orange stick, remove dirt from under your nails. Then take some cuticle cream, or rich moisturiser, and massage well around the nail using the ball of your thumb in a firm rotating movement. Using the flat end of an orange stick, gently ease back the cuticle.

Finish by massaging hand cream into your hands.

FEET TREAT

Your feet carry you around stuffed into socks and shoes and get very little thanks for it. So give them a treat occasionally with a pedicure. Start by soaking your feet in warm soapy, water and remove rough skin from heels, sides and soles of your feet with a pumice stone.

Dry your feet well, particularly between the toes. Now cut your nails squarely across the top, following the shape of your toe. Then smooth the edges with the coarse side of an emery board. Finish by repeating the routine used for hands with an orange stick and moisturiser.

Now you should be in condition all over!

TOTAL BEAUTY CARE

THE
THOMPSON
TWINS
MY GUY

FACE UP TO IT!

A face can give away a million secrets as you'll soon discover when you read our analysis...

The Cheek Of It

Those podgy cheeks of Simon Le Bon, don't just meen he's turning into a little piggy. They show he's got a sensitive character somewhere deep inside – you have to hunt to find it though – and that all he wants is to be loved and cared for.

That babyish face also means he's probably been a bit spoilt throughout his life and just loves to indulge himself, namely in his passion for sailing and his love of expensive clothes by top designer names.

He's also a whizz kid with girls, pretty confident and easy-going. But don't expect him ever to be faithful. That's just not part of his character. Watch out, Yasmin!

Hair's Fair

A full head of hair, apart from indicating pretty good health, also means that someone's clever, thoughtful and is often a real sign of success.

And Feargal Sharkey definitely lives up to that analysis.

But it also can mean a sort of Peter Pan approach to life where they just don't want to grow up to face the big, bad world.

Feargal's head also features a pretty strong brow, which reveals his determination to do well, and climb right to the top of the tree.

He's also someone who can be trusted with any problem and will be sure to spare time for anyone who needs his help.

Nosing Around

That big hooter of Geldof's is a real character giveaway. Because it shows a person who's open and honest and who doesn't keep any secrets – a real big mouth to suit Bob's over-the-top personality.

It also shows an extrovert, someone who's not in the slightest bit afraid of doing or saying exactly what they think.

A large nose also reveals a kind and generous streak to someone's nature.

Eyes Right

These close set eyes of Holly Johnson make us a bit suspicious.

And as they're slightly deep set as well, we definitely wouldn't trust him with any really important secrets.

Because his type of eyes indicate a very devious type of guy, one who'll use anything and anybody to get their own way in life.

They can also show great care with money, so never ask him for a loan – he'll only say no.

Which car for

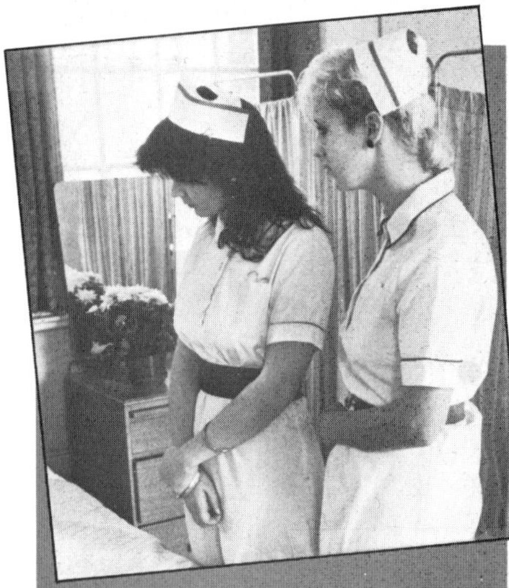

Nurses require dedication and a strong sense of duty.

It's not easy knowing what job to do when you leave school. How do you know what you'll be good at and enjoy so you'll know what to try and work towards? Take MY GUY's special careers test to discover what line of work you're most suited to...

1 If you're thrown into a family party your reaction is to:
a. Have a great time talking to all those relations you haven't seen for years?
b. Entertain all those little nieces and nephews?
c. Circulate while making a mental note of how much weight Aunty Rose has put on, and what an unflattering hairstyle your older cousin has gone and had cut?
d. Slip upstairs and beat your uncle hollow on the new computer game dad bought?

2 An unexpected treat – mum wins a few quid on the Bingo and gives you £10 extra pocket money. Do you:
a. Take a gang of mates out for a burger nosh?
b. Add to your collection of pets by buying an exotic bird/rabbit/fish?
c. Go and have a completely new haircut and colour?
d. Save it towards that space-age high tech gadget you've been longing to get your hands on?

3 At school your favourite subjects are:
a. English and group discussions on everyday subjects?
b. Biology, domestic science and health care talks?
c. Gym, games and art?
d. Most of the science subjects along with maths?

4 Last time you babysat for a neighbour you:
a. Asked a couple of mates round because you couldn't stand the thought of being by yourself all evening?
b. Got into trouble for keeping the baby up half the evening playing with it?
c. Took the opportunity of a night alone to give yourself a beauty treat – a face pack?
d. Had a great time reading a magazine you found on computers?

5 Getting a Saturday job can be hard enough – but if you could choose what you'd do to earn some extra cash you'd:
a. Work in a busy shop or snack and burger bar?
b. Find something where you came into close contact with young kids, like a baby shop – or animals, like a pet shop?
c. Go straight for a job in a hairdresser's, gym or on a cosmetic counter?
d. Work in a computer shop?

Typing may sound dull but it can lead to greater things.

6 Your best pal moves miles away, but you swear you're going to keep in contact. But when it comes to keeping your promise you:
a. Stick to your word. Your letters aren't that regular, but when you write one, boy, is it long and juicy?
b. You only remember important things like birthdays?
c. You'd like to write often, but you just hate writing letters?
d. You never get round to writing, but you love to have a really long 'phone call a few times a year?

7 Your boyfriend fell off his motorbike and broke his leg. When you go to visit him in hospital you:
a. Spend a lot of the visiting hour chatting to one of the student nurses you've seen down at the disco?
b. Take him a big cuddly pink teddy and wonder why he breaks into a hot flush and tries to hide under the sheet?
c. Pamper him with lots of butch smelly gifts?
d. Take your pocket Scrabble so you can beat him while he's down?

8 If you're suddenly stuck in a crisis you:
a. Panic until you get help, and then you act like nothing's happened?

eer's you?

b. Cope amazingly well. Somehow a panic brings out the best in you?
c. Go to pieces and end up feeling a right twit?
d. Get angry with yourself because the situation can't be solved by logical thinking?

9 If you were stranded on a desert island your one luxury would have to be:
a. Your photograph album with all the silly shots of you and your daft mates so you wouldn't get too lonely?
b. Your little pet dawg?
c. A mirror and make-up bag. You couldn't have all those tropical birds looking at you make-up free?
d. A calculator, so you could set yourself lots of mathematical exercises – like how many Pina Coladas you could make from all those coconuts?

TEST WHAT THE FUTURE HOLDS FOR YOU!

Computers will provide the jobs for the future.

score

Mostly a's
You're very outgoing and sociable – in fact you hate being on your own. You're good at getting on with other people, chatting and making them feel at ease, so you'd be best aiming for the kind of job where you're dealing with the general public every day. Luckily there are lots of opportunities in these fields – from working in a shop (and that doesn't just mean being an assistant, but working your way up to be a manageress or a buyer) to being a receptionist or working in the tourist or catering world.

Mostly b's
Young children, babies and animals seem to be your main loves, so why not plump for a job working with one of these? Nursing, or training as a nanny is a good idea. You'll need school qualifications to study further – either to be a nurse or study something like zoology, so keep working at school.

Mostly c's
Lucky for you that the fashion, keep-fit and beauty market is expanding because you seem cut out to work at making others look and feel good. There are plenty of courses you can go on to get experience and qualifications for these types of jobs.

Mostly d's
You're a new technology whizz kid in the making – just the thing to be when every factory and office will soon have some kind of computer as a vital part of the business.
You like sitting down and working out problems, and although you like to socialise when you're in the mood, it doesn't bother you to be working on your own – just you and your computer!

DON'T PLAY

WITH HER HEART

If you knew Eva, like I knew Eva, you probably wouldn't have known her at all. But then, how many of us did? And it hurts me to admit that, because generally I think of myself as the sort of guy who knows just about everything, and has everyone sussed, right down to the last secret vice.

See, I get around. In the offices, I mean. I know every girl here, and I reckon I've been out with every one between the ages of sixteen and twenty-six.

In fact, I was saying just that, when Danny, who's a bit of a liberty-taker, suddenly piped up.

"Except for Eva Harrow. You've never been out with *her.*"

"Who'd want to?" Jacko chipped in.

"I dunno . . . she's not bad-looking, up close," I murmured.

"Bet you couldn't, Steve!" Danny said.

"Couldn't what?"

What started as a date could have ended in true love . . .

"Get a date with the Dark Horse."

"Wanna bet?"

"Didn't I say so?"

And that's how the whole thing started, me and little Eva.

LUCKY

My lucky break came – as it always does – the day I saw her poring over a glossy book about Spain.

"Like Spain, do you?" I murmured.

"Mmmm!" she said. That's all I'd ever heard her say.

"Going on your hols there?" I asked, next time I saw her.

"Mmm," she murmured.

"Well, I'm the expert, kiddo. Anything you want to know you just ask me!" I winked at her.

"Like Spanish food – paella and squid and all that? Well, don't suppose you've had much chance to try it, but tell you what – there's a Spanish restaurant just opened in Carrick Place. Saturday night's Fiesta Night. I'll book a table for two, this Saturday, if you fancy coming along!"

She raised her grey wobbly eyes from the book.

"Mmm!"

"You'll come?"

"Mmm," she agreed.

"How much was that bet again?" I demanded later, grinning successfully at Danny the Wimp.

"A fiver. Get away, you've never got a date with it!"

It was hard-going at first, even though I had to admit the kid looked not too bad at all in a Spanish-style dropped waist dress in flaming red.

Then, I hit the magic formula. It was after she'd ordered from the menu reading out the Spanish names carefully, biting her tongue and clicking her teeth over some of them. The Spanish waiter beamed.

"I shouldn't bother," I confided in her. "You've been reading them phrase-books, haven't you? Take it from me, you don't need the lingo. Just say the English loud enough and slow enough. They understand. Listen, there's nothing I don't know about Spain. Let me tell you . . ."

And I did. It perked her up, no end.

She smiled as I told her all about my holidays. There was something about Eva's attentiveness, that got me, right there.

Maybe it was when she started to join in the singing, in a low husky voice that sounded like warm Spanish nights. Or maybe it was when she stood up on the dance floor, clapped her hands, stamped her heels.

"You've been taking lessons, haven't you?" I goggled at her when she sat down at the table.

"Guess so," she said.

Better than mmm, see? We were getting somewhere.

And I was getting into deeper water than I'd ever drowned in.

"Eva," I murmured, slipping my arm round her shoulders as I stumbled out beside her, "We gotta do this again. Soon, Wednesday?"

"I'm going to Spain on Monday," she said, sliding out from under my arm and hopping onto a passing bus.

"When you come back, then?" I yelled, as the beautiful flame-red figure flickered and died in the distance.

She hadn't replied. Just grinned a quirky and fascinating grin.

MAGIC

I missed her. Badly. She'd brought back all the magic of the Spanish sun. I cursed the fact that I'd booked for a fortnight's Singles holiday in Aviemore, this year. I needed to hold her hand, look into her eyes and . . .

"When's Eva back?" I asked the girls at work, after ten days or so.

"Back?" Deb giggled. "Back? She was never all here, was she?"

"Back? She's back, Stevo," Karen said nudging the other two. "Where she belongs!"

"Huh?"

"Never said a word, not a word," Sasha murmured. "You'd've thought she'd've said. Still, she never said anything. Only to the boss. He told us yesterday. Eva's gone back home, to Spain. Getting married, next week, and all. Eva Haro . . . suppose it is a Spanish sort of name, really."

"Suppose we never really knew her." Deb said.

Suppose we didn't. Me, least of all . . .

HOOKED ON HOROSCOPES?

ARE YOU STARSTRUCK?

Do you reckon it's all in the stars? Try our quiz, and find out whether you may be taking it all a bit *too* seriously!

1 Oh, dear – your day's horoscope in a newspaper foretells bad luck. Do you:
(a) Have a good laugh?
(b) Feel tempted to stay in all day?
(c) Take no notice, since you've been barricaded in your bedroom ever since your magazine horoscope for the week said you were in for a dodgy time?

2 If you've failed your exam, do you think:
(a) It can't be your fault – it's just that Mercury was in the wrong sign when you were born?
(b) Well, your horoscope said you'd have a bad month, career-wise?
(c) Maybe it had something to do with the fact that you left your revision until two hours before the exam?

3 You've just discovered your new boyfriend's birthdate – do you:
(a) Feel a bit worried, as you never did trust Leos?
(b) Make a note of the date, so you'll be sure to buy him a birthday present?
(c) Rush home to cast his astrological chart, so you can see whether he's the dark stranger your horoscope said *you'd* marry?

4 This week's horoscope has promised you financial gain! Do you think it means:
(a) The horoscope writer must be running out of ideas, since you've notices that five of the other zodiac signs have been promised more or less the same thing this week?
(b) You'll hear that you've won the contest you entered?
(c) You'll finally manage to prise out that £1 coin that's wedged between your floorboards?

5 You and your boyfriend have been quarrelling a lot – so do you think:
(a) Everyone knows that people born under his star sign are a moody, awkward bunch?
(b) It's a personality clash – probably caused by the fact that his sign isn't supposed to get on with yours?
(c) Maybe you shouldn't have two-timed him for his best mate while he was on holiday?

6 Now for the hard one. Do you think a cusp is:
(a) The days that begin and end a zodiac sign period?
(b) A biscuit babies eat?
(c) Something astrological, but you've never been too sure what?

7 Do you believe a horoscope you read:
(a) To some extent – but you feel a bit dubious about it all when one magazine promises you a quite different week or month from that forecasted in another mag?
(b) Completely?
(c) About as much as you believe in Father Christmas, The Easter Bunny and a gypsy fortune teller at a fête?

8 Do you get really embarrassed when:
(a) You confidently tell a new friend you're sure she's a Gemini – and get it wrong?
(b) Your mates catch you reading your "stars" in My Guy?
(c) You read your boyfriend his horoscope, and he laughs at you?

SCORE

	(a)	(b)	(c)
1.	0	5	10
2.	10	5	0
3.	5	0	10
4.	0	10	5
5.	10	5	0
6.	10	0	5
7.	5	10	0
8.	10	0	5

0 – 25: You might glance at your horoscope occasionally, but if you do, you feel annoyed with yourself – and, anyway, you soon forget what you've read! You're a down-to-earth person, with a healthy cynicism about anything in the fortune-telling line. You believe in making your own fate, not having it all sorted out for you. You'll be the person *you* want to be, not the person your zodiac sign says you're supposed to be!

30 – 60: You're quite interested in astrology, but on the whole you're too sensible to let anything you've read on the subject worry or excite you for long. You're not entirely sure you believe in it all. Be careful, though, as you could be in danger of letting astrology cloud your judgement and get in the way of your relationships at times.

65 – 80: Astrology should be just a bit of fun. You're taking it far too seriously – and this could be dangerous. Even astrology experts who thoroughly believe in their subject will admit that a prediction or a zodiac sign personality analysis is far from being always 100% accurate. It's dangerous to let what you believe is "fate" run your life. You've got free will, and there's no reason why you should be exactly the person some astrology article says you should be. Work on faults – don't just accept they're inevitable because of your star sign. Don't let astrology prejudice you – make your own decisions about people.

THE FLAME HAD DIED-BUT WAS THERE STILL A SPARK?

She felt trapped and she had to get away

EVERYTHING MUST CHANGE

"This isn't something I've rushed into"

COMPLETE PHOTO STORY

So Sue went round to see him.
. . .MIKE, WHY ARE YOU DOING IT?
WHY AM I DOING WHAT?
YOU KNOW DAMN WELL.
HOW CAN YOU GET ENGAGED TO SOMEONE YOU'VE KNOWN FOR JUST A MONTH?
IT'S VERY EASY, YOU JUST ASK THEM AND IF THEY SAY YES YOU BUY A RING.
YOU'RE NOT DOING IT TO SPITE ME, ARE YOU? BECAUSE IF YOU ARE, THAT'S STUPID. YOU'LL REGRET IT FOR THE REST OF YOUR LIFE.
WHY ARE YOU SO INTERESTED IN MY WELFARE ALL OF A SUDDEN?
WHY SHOULDN'T I BE? WE WERE TOGETHER FOR TWO YEARS.
SO YOU STILL CARE FOR ME?
OF COURSE I DO. MAYBE IN SIX MONTHS TIME WHEN I'VE SORTED MYSELF OUT WE COULD HAVE GOT BACK TOGETHER, WHO KNOWS. BUT WE CAN'T IF YOU'RE ENGAGED.
ACTUALLY, I HAVEN'T GOT ENGAGED AT ALL. THERE'S NO ONE CALLED SANDRA. I MADE HER UP.
WHAT?
I PLACED THE ANNOUNCEMENT THREE TIMES BEFORE YOU NOTICED IT. I HAD TO FIND OUT IF YOU REALLY DID CARE WHAT HAPPENED TO ME. COME ON, FORGET THE SIX MONTHS.
MICHAEL!
I THOUGHT YOU SAID I'D LOST MY SENSE OF HUMOUR.
I THOUGHT YOU HAD.
He didn't know how long they would stay together, but for the moment Mike had got Sue back.
THIS TIME I WON'T LET YOU GO.
And that's all he wanted.

FIGHT FOR ME!

"Let's have a coffee before we go to the pictures," I suggested.

The guy, Darren, nodded. He was a right nurd, as expected. Kelly, in the office, had fixed me up with him.

I tugged at his arm, and pulled him into 'Snax'.

"Best cup of coffee in town," I told him. Greasiest hell-hole in town, if the truth be known. But it was Friday night, and on Friday night Ray usually poled up there, about seven, to see what was going on. In the good old days, he'd taken me with him. But the good old days had ended, a fortnight before, when I'd caught him with this punky girl at the disco.

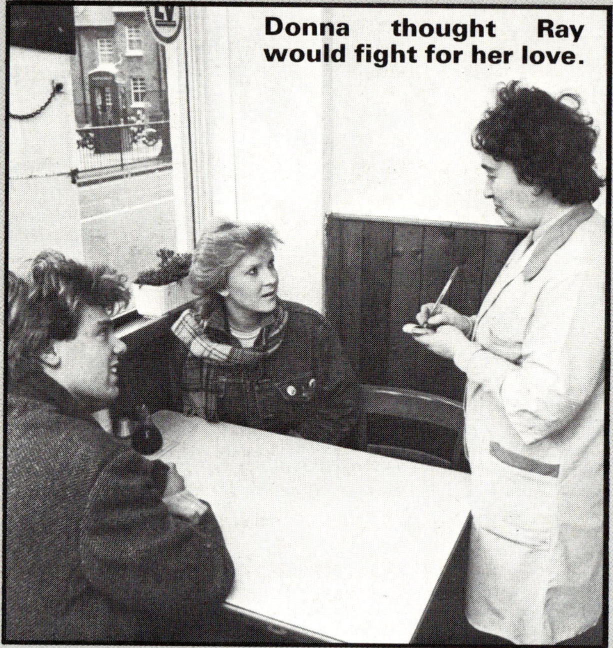

Donna thought Ray would fight for her love.

Darren went up to the counter, and I trailed behind, just close enough to show the staring eyes that I was with him. Joe, behind the counter, muttered to me, "I don't want no trouble, Donna."

"What trouble?" I asked, all innocent.

"What did he mean?" Darren asked, following me to a seat.

"Oh, nothing," I grinned, remembering.

TEMPER

We'd had some real battles in Snax, Ray and I. I suppose that's fair enough when you put a temper like his together with a temper like mine.

Darren stirred his coffee and stared at me. I ignored him. Ray was walking in, and my eyes were with him, all the way.

"We'd better get a move on. The film starts in ten minutes," Darren murmured.

"Plenty of time!" I said.

Ray hadn't seen me yet. But he would, soon. I stroked Darren's hand, and looked into his eyes.

"So, tell me about yourself," I murmured, invitingly, and Ray turned, and saw us. Timing. I'd got it just perfect.

"I'm from Newcastle, I'm unemployed, and looking for work down here. And if you don't mind me asking, why are you coming on hot and strong, all of a sudden?"

I didn't like that last remark. There was something sharp and far too canny in it.

"Oh, it's just that someone's looking at me, and I want him to know that I'm with you, that's all!" I said sweetly.

"Someone you know?" Darren asked.

"Oh . . . I've seen him around. He keeps asking me to go out with him," I lied.

Darren turned to look. Ray looked away.

"The guy in the leather bomber?" Darren asked.

I nodded.

"Oh," Darren muttered, his eyes narrowed.

I smiled encouragingly at him. "Your turn", he said.

"My turn?" I stammered.

"I've told you about me, Kelly said you work with her. That's all I know about you. More or less," he said.

Ray was looking straight at me, raising his eyebrows as much as to say, "Who's he?" I gave him a dirty look and turned back to Darren.

JOKER

"That guy's annoying me," I said.

"Oh yes?" he muttered.

"He keeps staring."

"So let's go. No point in hanging around if someone's annoying you."

But Ray had been watching the whole time. Now he loafed across.

"Hi, Donna," he muttered. "Who's this joker you're with?"

"None of your business," I sneered. "Darren, tell this guy to push off."

Darren just stood there, looking from Ray to me.

"Go on then," Ray suggested, poking him in the chest with one sharp finger. "Tell me to push off. Try it. Just try it!"

I almost choked with excitement. I couldn't believe that things were going so perfectly. Two guys, fighting over me.

Darren pushed the hair back out of his eyes, and then pushed Ray's hand away.

"Don't threaten me . . ." he started to say.

I nudged Ray, encouragingly. "Don't threaten him. He's a real hard case."

But, out of the blue, Darren glanced at me, and snapped, suddenly.

"You. I've got you sussed!"

Ray looked bewildered.

"You used to go out with her, right?" he asked.

Ray grunted.

"And now you think she's going out with me? Wrong! We're on a blind date. I'm supposed to take her to the movies, but she's sidetracked me into here.

"Obviously trying to wind you up. And me. We're both getting a bad deal out of this, mate. She's trying to use me. So, if you want her, you're welcome."

He stretched out his hand, Ray shook it.

"She's not worth it," Ray agreed.

"What?" I exploded, bursting into tears.

"What movie are you going to see?" Ray asked.

"Sylvester Stallone," Darren told him.

"Mind if I tag along with you. I fancy seeing that."

They walked out together. Ray made some sarky comment. Darren laughed. I flopped back into my seat, buried my head in my hands and cried. One step ahead of everyone? Not this time.

Name: DONNA BENSON Age: 17

Birthplace: ROCHDALE

THE CASEBOOK
20th OCT 1986

X-WORD EXTRAS!

This gruesome twosome should give you a few clues.

ACROSS
3. What Amii knocked on (4)
6. Careless whisperer (6)
7. The boys Wham! had a hit with (3)
8. Howard's pearl container (5)
9. Where you'd find Mick and David dancing (6)
10. One played with Annie's heart (5)
11. Coconut kid! (6)
14. Police drummer (7)
16. Weller's sticky old band (3)
17. Lynott and Moore were out in them (6)
18. Ms. Ullman's guy (2)
21. Ex-Beatle drummer (5)
22. *Close (To The Edit)* band … Of Noise (3)
24. Tatty cat on a Duran album (5)

DOWN
1. This Beatle classic wasn't made today! (9)
2. Wham! took a liberty with this No. 1! (7)
3. Direction to go for goodbye girl's guys (4)
4. He's apt to sing suddenly! (5)
5. This guy and his soul band had a hit with *Shaft* (4)
7. Nick Heyward wore one for a blue day (4,3)
12. *Tahiti* was a hit for him (5)
13. Paul Young hit, *Come Back And…* (4)
15. What Limahl's story never had (6)
17. Big Country's fields were full of it (4)
19. Where Bruce was born (1,1,1)
20. Transport for The Cool Notes (3)
23. Colour Field's front man (inits)

ANSWERS
ACROSS: 3. Wood; 6. George; 7. Bad; 8. Shell; 9. Street; 10. Angel; 11. Creole; 14. Stewart; 16. Jam; 17. Fields; 18. My; 21. Starr; 22. Art; 24. Tiger.
DOWN: 1. Yesterday; 2. Freedom; 3. West; 4. Ocean; 5. Eddy; 7. Blue Hat; 12. Essex; 13. Stay; 15. Ending; 17. Fire; 19. USA; 20. Car; 23. TH (Terry Hall).

Simon le Bon should help you with our x-word

ACROSS
4. Geldof's lady (5)
7. Nik Kershaw's Don (7)
9. Sade's surname (3)
10. Main man with Blancmange (4,6)
11. Beatles' Classic, *…Loves You* (3)
14. Colour Field's vocalist (5)
15. They told William that it was really nothing (6)
17. Arcadian singer (5)
18. Jacksons' classic, *….. It On The Boogie* (5)
20. The colour for Mr. Gartside (5)
21. Phil Collins was the drummer with this band (7)
23. Pete Wylie's mighty combo (3)

DOWN
1. A regal band (5)
2. Harold Faltermeyer's hit (4,1)
3. Marc Almond told them of Johnny (7)
5. King likes the taste of these (5)
6. Jools' reformed band (7)
8. Adam had a hit with this Prince (8)
12. Where Bruce Springsteen was born (1,1,1)
13. This moon was sung about by Echo and co. (7)
14. High energied Evelyn (6)
16. Stevie had a part time one (5)
19. A Duran Taylor (4)
22. He was the owner of a bird of paradise (inits)

ANSWERS
ACROSS: 4. Yates; 7. Quixote; 9. Adu; 10. Neil Arthur; 11. She; 14. Terry; 15. Smiths; 17. Simon; 18. Blame; 20. Green; 21. Genesis; 23. Wah.
DOWN: 1. Queen; 2. Axel F; 3. Stories; 5. Tears; 6. Squeeze; 8. Charming; 12. USA; 13. Killing; 14. Thomas; 16. Lover; 19. Andy; 22. SW (Snowy White).

ARE YOU A REAL ROMANT

1 Do you think this lad at a bowling alley is saying:
(a) "Not bad for your first lesson, Miss Bristow, but next time, try letting go of the ball *before* it hits the end of the alley!"
(b) "So you hold the ball like this . . . why, your hands – they're so small and soft!
(c) "When I'm this close to you, Linda, I – I get the wildest thoughts!"

2 This bride doesn't seem too happy on her wedding day! Do you reckon she's saying to the groom:
(a) "No, Simon, I can't marry you – I've realised I still love Tony!"
(b) "What do you *mean,* Dad's found he had no film in the video camera during the ceremony?"
(c) "I warned you I get hay fever from carnations – now I'm legally married to a Mr Atchoo! Simpson!"

3 It looks as though there could be trouble coming up here! What do you think this girl's saying to the boy as she opens the door to the other girl?
(a) "Steve, will you get off that phone? Your girlfriend's here!"
(b) "It's someone from next door – she says you've just played your Madonna LP through 15 times, and if you must play music that makes the floor virbrate, could you at least change the record?"
(c) "S-Steve? W-what's going on? This girl says she's your girlfriend – but you're engaged to me!"

4 It doesn't look as though the girl on the right is any too pleased about the way her date is going! Do you think her friend is saying:
(a) "Don't sulk, Deb, we'll go to see *Rambo* next week, okay?"
(b) "All right, yours is a bit weird, but we'll swap partners half way through the evening, okay?"
(c) "Don't worry, you'll get back together again – it was just a small lovers' tiff!"

Some people just can't help reading romance into any situation! Find out whether you're a head-in-the-clouds romantic, or as down-to-earth as Yorkshire pud!

IC ?

5 Here's a happy little family group! What do you think Dad's saying to the young man?
(a) "Welcome to the family! I hope you and my daughter will be very happy!"
(b) "Congratulations, my boy! Three maths 'O' level attempts was a lot, but I knew you'd get it in the end!"
(c) ". . . So, as your Amanda's first boyfriend to last longer than one date, I'm giving you a free evening out for two at McDonalds!"

6 This bloke looks a bit down-in-the-mouth – what do you reckon his office-mate is saying to him!
(a) "I know you're heartbroken about Jenny just now, but remember *I'll* always be here, whenever you need me!"
(b) "I wouldn't hand in your resignation too hastily, Trev, I don't think the boss really noticed that you got carried away at the Christmas party and serenaded his wife with *Nellie Dean*?
(c) "... and I'm sure she'll come back if you apologise for keeping her waiting outside the wrong cinema for two hours . . ."

7 These two lads look a bit stroppy – what do you think the girl is saying to them?
(a) "I don't know why you two can't just accept that you don't both agree about Everton's chances, and forget it!"
(b) "Look, do you two think this is really the time or the place to rehearse a fight scene in your club's production of *West Side Story*?
(c) "Please don't fight over me – I'm not worth it!"

8 What do you think this boy is saying to his girlfriend?
(a) "Not bad, love, but I think the other sort of foundation suited you better"
(b) "Let me look at you... why, you're beautiful!"
(c) "Gosh, that's a nasty spot – do you want some antiseptic for it?"

SCORE

	(a)	(b)	(c)
1.	0	5	10
2.	10	5	0
3.	5	0	10
4.	10	5	0
5.	10	5	0
6.	10	0	5
7.	5	0	10
8.	5	10	0

0 – 25: Heavy romance rather embarrasses you. You've got a crazy, zany sort of sense of humour, and like to laugh at anything you think is a bit corny or absurd. What you really like is fun, and even if you're in quite a close relationship, you're a bit wary of what you think of as "soppy talk", or of openly showing that the relationship is romantic.

30 – 60: You've got a romantic element, but you like your romance presented in a down-to-earth way. Low-key, modern-style romance appeals to you more than the traditional soft-focus variety does. Relationships that grow and develop gradually suit you better than "love at first sight" ones, which you don't really believe in. You're inclined to read romantic-type relationships into the scenes you see – but you don't easily see heavy romance.

65 – 80: Yes, you're a real soft-hearted, head-in-the-clouds romantic! You'd see romance even in the dullest of situations. Be careful that your desire for romance isn't leading you to see it in relationships where it doesn't really exist, or you could get hurt. You tend to fall for boys too quickly, too heavily and too often, and are all too likely to be used and disappointed.

THEY'VE GOT PROB

MIKE READ'S EGO . . .

"Look, mate, to be honest with you, I don't really know why I'm here. I mean, it's not as though I've even got a problem, or anything. Just the opposite, I'd say. After all, I've got a good job at Radio One in which I tell the millions of daily listeners lot of interesting things – about me.

"I feed them information on who's the current world's biggest sex symbol – me; who's the most gifted performer both in song and with guitar – me; and who's got the sexiest smile in the business – me.

"Oh, how the peasants love it, they adore me, scream for me, write me endless love letters – you **must** have heard them, I read every one out on air. They adore my cheery patter, my witty ad libs – not pre-planned at all, you understand – and modest demeanor.

"You see, I've always been a somewhat humble chap. As I said to my good pals George and Andy just the other . . ."

If you don't mind, Mr Read . . .

"No please, don't bother with the formalities, Sir Michael will do perfectly well, and *do* try to remember, peasant, that *I'm* paying for your time and I don't take kindly to having a little non-entity like you butting in on **MY** floorshow. So shut it.

"Now, ah yes, to be or not to be,

that is the question. You know, I've always considered myself to have the makings of a fine Shakespearean character actor. I'd give old Lol Olivier a good run for his money anyday – it's just a case of finding the time. I mean everyone seems to want a part of me as it is.

It's the same with the singing, not that I'd want to steal the show from my mate Cliff – anyway he needs the money more than I do. Bet he'd like to be in my shoes though . . ."

Zzzzzzzzzz . . .

MADONNA'S MEGALOMANIA . . .

"I wanna be bigger than God. I'm GONNA be bigger than God – and that's just my aim for this month. I'll do it, too. Y'see, I always get what I want an' I don't give a damn who gets kicked aside in the process. Who needs people anyway? I just need me.

"Y'know I've got this one ambition left – until next week, that is. When I get up on stage at the Academy Awards next year, to accept my Oscar for Best Actress, you understand, I'll have one thing to say. I've got my speech planned all ready for the

call-up. 'Thank you, Madonna, for being such a wonderful person. Praise be to God – me.' That's all. Isn't that cool?

"Y'know, I've been thinking of going into politics – after all, Ronnie did it and he was only a two bit B-Movie actor. I'd make a great President, all that power, all those people acting upon my every command . . . or maybe I'll shoot over here to little old England 'n' marry one of your Princes. That Charles is *so* good-looking – it'd be a great career move.

Don't you think you're over-looking one small point? He's already married.

Just imagine what a conversation between our favourite pop stars and their analysts might sound like. Then read on and find out . . .

LEMS!

PRINCE'S PARANOIA . . .

"Just don't look at me, Okay? Stand over there, face that wall with your hands above your head, and don't move a muscle. Okay, Chuck, check him out for hidden bugging devices, '45 revolvers, flick knives and green striped socks. I can't bear to be in the same room as anyone who's wearing green striped socks, ever since this photographer guy tried to take a shot of me at 6.32p.m. on 19 July 1983, Long Island. He had green striped socks on and it turned out he was carrying a candy bar shotgun in his Levi's pocket. Said it was for his kid back home, but I know different. He was out to get me, you understand? He wanted to kill me!!"

Er, quite, Mr Rogers. Now tell me, how long is it since you've been afflicted with this fear of persecution?

"Hey, don't get me wrong, I don't have a fear of persecution, it's just that everyone's out to get me... "They resent me for my greatness, for my affinity with God, for the fact that I've been placed on this earth for a Purpose ..."

Oh, I can well believe that, Mr Rogers . . .

"Hey, what are you gettin' at? You implyin' I'm some kind of crank? A weirdo? It's cos I'm so short, ain't it? Pick on a guy because he's shorter than you. And that's another thing . . . you think I actually *like* wearing these godamn platforms? I've got to get noticed somehow, haven't I? You tryin' to give me some kind of inferiority complex? Chuck . . . shoot him."

WE'RE HERE TO HELP

NIK KERSHAW'S HEIGHT . . .

"I think it must've started when I suddenly noticed that all the guys at work were flashing their Burton bags while my mum was still dragging me around Mothercare. That's when it finally hit home that I'd always be standing on crab apple boxes just to even be nose to chest to the stumpiest girlfriend.

"Until then I'd hoped (and prayed – every night) that either this was all a horrible dream I'd soon wake up from, or that I'd be one of the late developers who suddenly shot up to 6ft 2in on their 16th Birthday. No such luck, 16 came and went and I was still acting a part in Gulliver's Travels. I tried everything: sleeping suspended from the bedroom light bulb; planting myself on a Fison's GroBag for three weeks; even becoming the first lad with a three foot Mohican – and **still** I was under 4ft 7in (or that's what it feels like, anyway).

"Do you realise I was wearing stacked heels way before all these 70's glam rock stars got into it. 'Course, as soon as they did, I was back to square one again – short. Or 'of little length' as my missus puts it."

Don't you think you're exaggerating the issue a little here.

I have a tape measure here – perhaps an actualisation on your height will be the first step toward solving this problem. Now just stand up, Mr. Kershaw...

"I **am** standing up."

Oh.

THE LOVE GAME

Alli had worked out a perfect scheme to win back Glen's love . . .

I was up at the crack of dawn on The Day. I raced down the stairs in my sleepshirt, stupidly excited. I mean, I know exactly what Valentines I'd get. But only the newspaper lay on the doormat, no post, nothing.

For a moment, I had this dreadful sickening fear that something had gone wrong before I pulled myself together and told myself that nothing could possibly go wrong.

The scheme was great. I'd thought it up, so it had to be. Then I remembered that the postman was always late on Valentine's Day, like last year, for instance, when Glen's very first shy proposition had arrived just as I was belting down the front path on my way to school.

It had been the best February in my living memory. And the next seven or eight months of drifting at Glen's side had been pretty good, too. And then there was Christmas. And since then, I'd grown up enough to realise that all guys were pigs, Glen included, and that the only way to deal with them was to rub their noses in it. That's what I planned to do, this Valentine's Day.

I leaned against the bathroom door. Nothing happened.

"Lin, are you in there?"

"Won't be long," she gurgled.

CRIED

She'd been gurgling for weeks and weeks, ever since she'd met Michael at work. She was a great disappointment to me, nowadays, was my big sister. In the days before she got Love, the way some people get The Black Death, she'd have been with me all the way, listening to the accounts of how I'd found Glen in the arms of Rachel Eaton, agreeing with me that mistletoe was no excuse, and that any guy stupid enough to fall for that blonde brick wall deserved to be finished with dramatically.

But, when I'd cried all over her, she'd only been capable of gurgling, "Are you sure you've done the right thing, Alison?" as if she were on Glen's side instead of mine.

Well, he'd be absolutely certain, after this Valentine's Day, that none of his feeble whining and wheedling and his lame excuses would cut any ice with me. Not when I flaunted my three Valentine Cards in front of him at school, three beautiful sloppy Valentine Cards, all in different handwriting, all from different areas of the city. He'd soon realise that I wouldn't have him back. No way.

"Lin, you *did* post my Valentines?" I yelled through the bathroom door.

"Uh huh!" she gurgled.

Three more times I ran downstairs, thinking that I heard a rattle in the letterbox. I'd told Lin to get them into the first post the day before. I'd explained that I wanted three of her mates at the office to write the address on the cards – Lin's handwriting was too much like mine, and Glen would suss that something funny was going on.

"Lin!" I yelled up the stairs.

"Gawd, is that the time? Got to dash!" she breathed, flying down the stairs. "Look at this card from Mickey. Fantastic, isn't it?"

"You got it this morning?" I demanded. "The postman's been?"

"Yeah. 'Course!" she smirked.

"But what about *my* cards?"

"I posted them, honest."

Second post then. It wasn't good enough. How was I supposed to flaunt them in front of Glen, and make him fall on his knees in front of me, begging me to forget all the others and love him again? I brushed my teeth, angrily, smeared soap and water across my face, into my wet eyes and couldn't get the soap out. Honestly, that was why I looked as if I was crying on the way to school. Soap in my eyes.

"Hi, Alli. Let's see your cards, then," Rachel Eaton called out, as soon as I staggered through the school gates.

"Left them at home," I muttered.

"Oh!" she sneered. "That bad, were they?"

"And what about your card from Glen?" I sneered back. Two could play at that game.

She blushed. "Him? Who needs him?" she snarled. I had to smile. He had obviously conveniently forgotten her. Maybe he'd never really liked her. Maybe, just maybe, there was a grain of truth in his protests at the time that he didn't fancy her, and that she'd just thrown herself into his arms as I was passing by. Maybe?

"Hi, Allison," Glen murmured, tugging at my elbow.

CRAZY

I turned to face him. My heart went into its usual crazy flurry.

"Oh, hi," I muttered, casually through my beetroot blushes.

"Thanks..... thanks for believing me, at last. I've missed you so much. Let's start again," he said. Rachel Eaton's face was a picture of green slant-eyed envy.

"OK, then!" I agreed, trying not to show how wobbly I was going all over. He took me by the hand, and led me away. Then he produced my three Valentine cards.

"I recognised your writing. I was so pleased that you still cared..." he whispered.

So Lin had posted them after all. As usual, these days, she hadn't listened. She'd scrawled them all in her look-alike handwriting, and posted them to Glen!

Or maybe she had listened. Maybe she thought she knew best. Maybe, just maybe, she was right. Somehow, it felt right.

NICK
RHODES
MY GUY

Hair

Look this way for everything you need to know for a blooming barnet.

WHICH TYPE?

First, you need to determine your hair type and then find out the best way to treat it:

Oily: Hair looks limp, lank, and greasy. It's caused by sebaceous glands in the scalp working overtime and producing too much sebum.

Dry: Hair looks dry and lifeless, and is prone to splitting and breakage. It's the result of a lack of sebum, so the hair is unprotected against dehydration.

Normal: Lucky you, your hair is shiny and healthy, no problems here. This is due to a healthy internal structure, with just the right amount of sebum produced, and shows good care. Most of us can have 'normal' hair as long as we treat it well.

Combination: Hair is greasy at the scalp and dry and split at the ends. Hair is basically of a greasy type, but the sebum isn't reaching the ends of the hair shaft due to frequent washing and the overuse of blowdryers and other heated appliances.

WASH WASH

Wash your hair whenever you want to, using a shampoo suited to your hair type. With greasy hair use a mild shampoo, such as a baby, or frequent wash shampoo, and wash it as often as you like. Every day if you want to. Avoid harsh shampoos as these strip the hair of its essential oils and can stimulate the scalp into producing even more oil, or result in 'combination' hair.

In fact combination hair types also suit these gentle shampoos. When lathering up work well into your scalp and massage for a couple of minutes. However, avoid massaging if you've a greasy scalp as again this may lead to the production of even more sebum.

Always rinse your hair thoroughly, as a soapy residue will lead to a scaly scalp and those all too familiar white flecks on your shoulders. However, hair should not be 'squeaky' clean as this means your hair has been stripped of essential oils necessary to keep it healthy.

SHINE ON

All hair types should be treated to a conditioner, which smooths down the cuticle of the hair, a layer of scales overlappping each other rather like birds' feathers. With out-of-condition hair these scales are ruffled making the hair appear dull, and leaving it vulnerable to dehydration.

Conditioner helps to keep this cuticle smoothed down, producing shiny healthy hair.

But it should be remembered that conditioner is used to help 'keep' the hair in good condition and once it is damaged a conditioner can do little to mend split hairs.

Greasy and combination hair types will only need conditioner applied to the ends of the hair as sebum is the hair's natural protection. However, there are now conditioners which treat combination types by reacting differently to different areas of your hair.

Putting all the right lotions and potions on your hair isn't enough though and you should remember that hair is largely the result of a healthy say

well-balanced diet with plenty of vitamin B. So make sure you're getting enough eggs, wholegrains, yeast extracts (marmite), and organ meats, such as liver and kidney.

BRUSH WORK

Choose combs and brushes with smooth moulded teeth which won't scratch your scalp or damage your hair. Forget the old wives tale about brushing your hair 100 times a day, it's definitely not the way to beautiful hair – and in fact is more likely to damage it by causing friction which disrupts the cuticle, and irritates the scalp.

It's particularly important that you're careful when combing or brushing wet hair as, in this state, hair loses a lot of its elasticity, and so is vulnerable. This means keeping comb and brush work to a minimum when hair is wet.

STYLE COUNCIL

When hair has been washed and rinsed, gently squeeze out excess water and then wrap a towel around your hair, turban style and press against your hair to absorb more water. Do not rub hair with the towel. Leave hair to dry naturally for as long as possible, before using the hairdryer. For best results, always point the nozzle down the hair shaft so as not to ruffle the cuticle.

A handful of gel or mousse and your fingers can be used more effectively to get your hair to move in the direction you want. For softer styles, mousse is best. But for more structured or spikier styles which need a stronger hold, you'll find gel more effective. For more body, start by roughly drying hair with your head upside down.

Then, when you begin to style it, use your fingers to pull hair out at right angles to your scalp and apply heat to the roots. Short styles can be left to dry naturally and then mousse or gel can be used to coax the style into place.

For natural waves, scrunch drying has proved very popular. To achieve this, pin up the top layers and, starting at the bottom, scrunch sections of hair in your palm and apply heat.

NEW MOVEMENT

There are a wide range of perms now available and they're full of conditioners, and so much kinder to your hair. Whether you want a headful of bubbly curls, loose waves or just a little body, go to a tried and tested hairdresser and take along a photo.

A perm is particularly good for oily hair as it will dry it out slightly and by lifting your hair away from the scalp, will help prevent the passage of oil down the hair shaft.

IN THE SHADE

There are three main types of colour to choose from: rinses which last for a couple of washes; semi-permanent tints which last for about six weeks; and permanent colour which lasts until you let it grow out, and so needs constant retouching at the roots when your natural colour grows through.

If you've decided on a permanent colour for your hair, then visit your hairdresser.

Rinses and semi-permanent colour, on the other hand, can be achieved quite sucessfully at home as long as you read the instructions very carefully and do a patch test on your hair first.

Now you've digested all this information you've no excuse not to have beautifully conditioned hair, with a style and colour to make other heads turn.

INDIVIDUAL *flair*

Make sure you don't merge with the crowd. Stand out by creating and individual look.

A sense of style can buy you more good looks than money can. Be an individual and you won't be a wall flower. Unleash your creative talents and make fashion fun not depressing. Want to know more, then dress this way:

MARKED PERSONAL

Having 'style' means knowing what suits you, and that means not only your figure but your personality and lifestyle as well. It's important you feel confident in what you're wearing and that confidence shines through. Be yourself. For instance, if you've got a party coming up, you may think about vamping it up in an expensive, figure-hugging dress. But is it right for *you*, will you feel comfortable in it? If you'd feel happier in a plain black crewe neck sweater and leggings, then wear them because you'll look better too. You'll exude a confident presence which is far more attractive than a very expensive dress. In fact, if you're wearing simple clothes and still manage to attract attention because what you're wearing is right for you, then others next to you who've got done up to the nines will feel overdressed!
Always let this personal style show through, whatever you buy. And don't try to copy piece for piece another person's look. Borrow ideas from others and then adapt them to suit yourself. Use others for inspiration but don't copy a style exactly.

EASY LIVING

Looking good should also look easy, and one of the rules of style is to make it look effortless. You may have spent ages putting your outfit together but only you should know. Avoid top-to-toe co-ordination, with everything matching and toning in, it looks contrived. You shouldn't look like you're taking dressing up too seriously. Clothes are to be enjoyed not cause tears. Using your imagination can make

fashion more fun and avoids finding yourself in the same outfit as someone else. This not only means looking at alternative sources for your clothes, such as second-hand shops, sports and boys departments and in chain stores, but how you put things together is also important. Keep an open mind and don't be afraid to break the rules to create an individual look. For instance, clash oranges, reds and pinks or wear black with dark brown or navy. Also try mixing satins and silks with denim or wear an Arran jumper over a lacey or chiffon dance skirt. Fashion doesn't dictate to us any more, become your own designer.
Today anything goes.

DESIGNS ON YOU

Use fashion magazines for inspiration. Don't just look through them for clothes to buy and then get depressed because they're too expensive or aren't available in your area. Instead study the feel of the clothes and predominant shapes, and take careful note of how they've been styled. Have sleeves been rolled back or left long and undone at the cuff, are collars done right up to the top or left open, are short skirts being worn with high shoes, or heavy, flat lace-ups, is the effect neat or scruffy? and so on.

IDENTITY

Pinch ideas from fashion pages but interpret them to suit yourself. Don't lift outfits straight off the fashion pages. Just because the model looks good rigged out from top-to-toe in designer wear doesn't mean it will suit you.
In fact, many designers prefer to see their clothes mixed in with others and are interested to see how they've been interpreted. They intend their clothes to be enjoyed and for the wearer to put her own identity on them rather than let the clothes rule them. So develop a style for yourself and be consistent, because what you haven't got in natural good looks you can make up for with style. And don't be afraid to attract attention, remember that when people stare at you it's a compliment, and it's when you merge in with everyone else and people don't notice you that it's time to get worried.

The Most Quo Man In The Universe...

Ever opened your gob, let a tirade of abuse and innuendo spill forth, then regretted it immediately? Many times, we're sure. Someone who has **no** regrets, though, is Dead Or Alive's Pete Burns.

Can *nothing* escape his cutting tongue and biting wit? Don't answer that... we'll just let the mouth speak for itself.

BOY GEORGE
Honestly, if it hadn't been for me there wouldn't have been a Boy George. I started dressing up in a female way at around thirteen. Before Boy George came along I was well known on the London fashion scene. We suffered because people thought I was trying to copy him.

SCHOOL
Burn down the lot of them. Kids need to learn how to handle life, not what to do with a decimal point.

HIS EDUCATION
I feigned a nervous breakdown at 14½ and never went back to school.

LIVERPOOL
Nowhere brings you down to earth quicker than a trip to Liverpool.

BRITISH RAIL
They have to give me a compartment to myself. If I sat in the carriage with everyone else, people would start to freak out.

PRINCE
That stupid Price doesn't even have to do an interview, they just put him on the front cover, he's so lucky. It's high camp but I wonder how long it'll wash with people. I think it's quite funny the way he gets all over everything. I think his music sounds a bit dated.

MARILYN
Marilyn came up to me one time and asked why I hated him, and I swear I've never said anything bad about the guy – he's scarcely crossed my mind. I don't know who made that one up for me!

able

THOMPSON TWINS
I hate the Thompson Twins, especially her with the hair.

WHAM!
I actually like Wham! They're just two toothpaste adverts with a microphone. Where do they get that tan lotion?

FAME
I hate people thinking they own a part of you, and once you've had a hit, some people think they can do what the hell they like – pulling your hair out, yanking you out of vans – and you're not supposed to react.

I can get really carried away, it's wonderful – blinds drawn full time, in bed with me chocolates saying, 'no, no, tell them I won't do it!' Last year I acted out every fantasy about every freaked-out, flapped-out Hollywood queen I ever heard of.

When we have hit records I could order a mink, really go potty, I'm a prize prat. I had a great time before and I'll go just the same way now. I bought a diamond nose ring, got me teeth capped with gold...

HUMOUR
One of my greatest attributes, it's what's got me here. I'm not blowing me own trumpet, but I really do have a great sense of humour. Put a machete through me head and I still would. In a business like this you need a sense of humour, you get trampled on so much. I can't function in a room full of po-faced miseries.

THE NOSE JOB
I was about to have the nose walloped on the day we found out that *You Spin Me Round* had entered the Top Forty, months after release, and they rang and said, 'You're on *Top Of The Tops*'. It would have meant paying a cancellation fee to the hospital if I put it off, so I went in anyway and just got the bandages off in time for TOTP. It takes ages to settle down so I went on looking like the Elephant Man.

I had the second after *Lover Come Back* – it hurt so much it brought tears to me ears. But it was worth it because I'd got bored with the old one; I thought I'd change the cherry on the doughnut. Nose jobs are rife in this industry but people think it's taboo to talk about them. I'm not bothered.

SPENDING MONEY
Spending money is almost my only vice, my only irresponsibility. I don't drink, smoke, take drugs. I wouldn't like to put my money up my nose, and when the cupboard's bare I have to go back and write more hits.

PETE'S IMAGE
I'm dead, dead boring! I don't like alcohol. I don't go in for the odd joint. I don't even like ciggies. And I'm a real stay-at-home. If only the world knew that this exotic, flamboyant, oddball creature can't stand parties 'cos the noise is too loud, and hates clubs 'cos they're claustrophobic, and likes nothing better than staying in for the evening simply watching videos with friends...

I used to put on me mum's stiletto boots and mime in the mirror to Nancy Sinatra. I wanted to grow up to be like her really. And here I am.

PETE'S MOUTH
My sharp-tongued nasty side isn't from bitterness or jealousy, it happens naturally. I just can't shut me mouth, I'm pretty stupid and irresponsible really – a prize prat!

The trouble is, if people ask me about something or someone I don't like, they know I'll give an honest answer. I don't mince my words and I admit I have a knack of hitting people's weak spots. I get verbal diarrhoea and I can see reporters trying to get me to say something I really shouldn't be saying, sitting there with their mouths open, waiting for a juicy quote.

THE FUTURE
The future? When I'm 55, I'll be just like Joan Collins. I'll still be caked in slap and they'll give me a part in a soap opera – as the bitch, of course.

WEST

IS BEST

So you think you know everthing there is to know about hunks of the decade, Go West.
Well, we bet you didn't know that:

20 THINGS YOU DIDN'T KNOW ABOUT THEM

1. Peter Cox went to Stanley Road Mixed Junior School in Richmond, Surrey.

2. Peter's dad was a magazine distributor for the United States Air Force.

3. Peter was in the Cubs – but left because it meant him missing his favourite TV programme, *Batman*, on a Wednesday evening.

4. Peter left home *and* school at the age of 17, and his first job was with an insurance company – Sun Life Assurance in Cheapside, London. He worked on group pension schemes.

5. Richard Drummie also left home at 17 – but his dad kicked *him* out!

6. At that age Richard suffered from insomnia so much that at one point all his eyelashes fell out through lack of sleep.

7. Richard turned his back on a highly paid career as a newspaper classified ad. manager in order to take up music.

8. Peter's first ever band was called Bodie.

9. And Richard's first band was called Free Agent.

10. The duo didn't even want to call themselves Go West. They preferred Partners In Crime or Moving Pictures – but there were already acts going by those names.

11. Before success hit them, Richard was once so hard up that he nearly ended up in prison.

12. They actually resorted to putting garlic in baked beans to make them taste more interesting.

13. Their very first live gig was when they recorded for Radio One's *In Concert*, while the second was a spot on *The Tube*.

14. The demos for *Call Me* and *We Close Our Eyes* were actually recorded in 1982 – three years before the latter was released as their debut single.

15. The video for said single was made by Godley and Creme and cost £90,000 to shoot.

16. That video was based (very loosely we might add) on the popular cult film *Rumblefish*.

17. Sylvester Stallone liked their music so much that he asked them to record a song for the soundtrack to the Rocky Four movie, *One Way Street*.

18. Richard is four years younger than Peter.

19. Peter thinks the most irritating thing about Richard is his lack of punctuality.

20. And Richard thinks that the most irritating thing about Peter is the way he shouts at Richard when he's late!

BOYS, THE STARS... AND YOU!

Suss out how to make your love life sparkle by following our star-scope guide. And we promise you'll be in heaven in 1987!

AQUARIUS

Okay, some people like to play it cool, but you can often verge on the iceberg temperature guide.

You're fine at the beginning of a romance when friendship's the key word, but the minute the mercury starts zooming up, you freeze.

You're one of the zodiac's best friends and often romance is a total turn-off. So next time, why not tell that guy to take it more slowly? You don't like to be pushed into a heavy love involvement too soon.

That way you won't be pressured against your will into a steady relationship with a boy.

Best 1987 bet: Leo.

PISCES

You've got the opposite problem to Aquarius. At the slightest hint of love, you imagine it's forever, and you're secretly planning the rest of your lives together. You're full of emotion and easily hurt so those romantic dreams often end up in pain for you.

So this year, don't imagine every date is the beginning of the real thing. Take it a week at a time and enjoy flirting and learning to understand guys. That way you'll learn to prevent those tearful anguished nights you know so well and just enjoy yourself.

Best 1987 bet: Scorpio.

ARIES

You're so full of energy, you often scare any eager guys away. Sit down, think before you speak and learn to listen to other people.

Yes, you can be great company but other people like to talk as well, so when you're out on that first date, ask the guy about himself, what hobbies he's interested in.

Then, once he's had a chance to chat, you can let go a bit and revert to holding court. And the crunch will come for you when what that guy's saying is much more interesting than your own conversation.

Best 1987 bet: Sagittarius.

TAURUS

You love any guy who'll spoil you to death, and feminism and the 80's just hasn't quite hit you.

You expect to be treated well, paid for and generally well looked after. But remember, most guys you meet just won't be able to afford all those frills, and even though they like you, might be put off asking for dates.

You're also a bit old-fashioned and set in your ways, and have high expectations from your relationships. So this year, go 50/50 money wise and love wise, relax a bit and you'll find love on your doorstep.

Best 1987 bet: Libra.

GEMINI

The more the merrier is your attitude to guys, and no matter what your mates might accuse you of, there doesn't seem much point in changing your attitude at the moment. One day you'll meet someone who's better than all your other fellas put together and you'll give up your flirting ways (or try to anyway). Just be careful you don't hurt those guys you flirt with. Some of them have a lot more sensitivity than you and could get bitter if you're not totally honest with them.

Best 1987 bet: Virgo.

CANCER

Like Pisces, you're full of doe-eyed romance and plan that cosy home together on the second date. You'll knit, cook and sew for the guy in your life until he gets so bored with another ver-

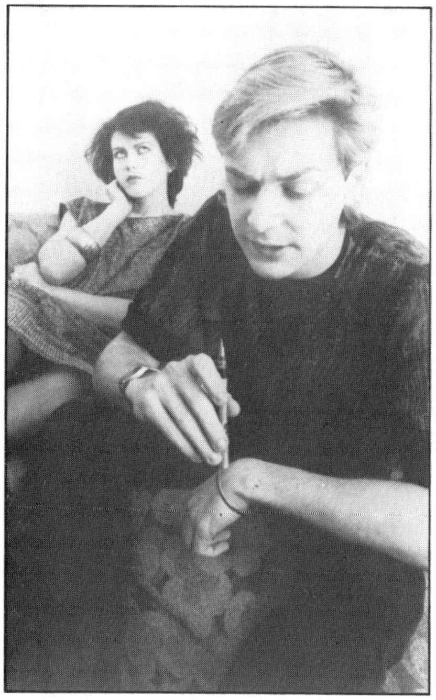

sion of Mum he'll go looking for excitement somewhere else. And then you'll be in total confusion about why he ditched you when you did so much for him.

So try to accept that the last thing on the minds of most guys you meet is boring domesticity and leave the knitting wool alone until you've settled into a steady relationship. Or simply don't talk about it! Take things as they come and you'll have more fun.

Best 1987 bet: Capricorn.

LEO

Is anyone out there good enough for you? And can they take those tantrums when you can't get your own way.

Leos are the life and soul of any party – provided they've organised it themselves, and have the choice of every guy there. This isn't to say Leos are selfish – they're not, but guys can often be put off by their demanding nature. Try to curb those temper tantrums and you'll find relationships a lot easier to cope with.

Best 1987 bet: Aquarius.

VIRGO

Often, you're the last amongst your circle of friends to form steady relationships or even be interested in boys, which is great, provided you're happy and contented. But often Virgos shy away from relationships because they're not sure of what to expect and scared of being hurt.

But this year, if you want some communication with boys, start by making friends.

Treat boys as people, not as strange objects totally different from you and simply learn to relax with them. The romance will develop and you'll become more sure of yourself.

Best 1987 bet: Pisces.

LIBRA

Librans are often the most attractive of the zodiac and have no trouble attracting people. But keeping them can be difficult once their 'couldn't care less' attitude begins to show.

Librans, however, believe in anything for an easy life and keeping the peace, and once their faults are pointed out will make attempts (not too strenuous, though) to rectify them.

This year, if you meet someone you're really interested in, why not show him and tell him you care? Just a few words will do.

Best 1987 bet: Gemini.

SCORPIO

Your major problem is your lack of trust of other people which in turn leads to jealousy.

If you don't know for sure someone's two-timing you, then you'll make it up in your own mind. And if you found out for sure, that jealousy would simmer over into real anger.

Try to calm down and take relationships at an easier pace.

You can be very dark and brooding which some guys simply can't handle at all.

Take a much lighter view of life from now on and you'll find more happiness coming your way.

Best 1987 bet: Virgo.

SAGITTARIUS

There's never enough time in the day or enough people to talk to and most guys find themselves dragged along behind you, forgotten in the rush.

Like Aries people, you're full of energy and others, who might be quieter, can't cope with it.

Take each task at a slower pace or you'll find out there's no one behind you when you decide you need them.

And that goes for friends as well as boyfriends.

Best 1987 bet: Gemini.

CAPRICORN

You're often misunderstood and seen as the very quiet, dark type. But once you relax you have a fantastic sense of humour and really do come alive.

But you need the right type of guy to make you be yourself and stop worrying about what other people think.

You're one of the zodiac's greatest worriers and any relationship will have you in a right old state. So stop panicking, you're just as good as the rest.

Best 1987 bet: Taurus.

STARSCOPE SPECIAL!

THE RIGHT BEAUTY QUIZ

Test out your beauty knowledge with our fact-finding quiz.

1. What is an exfoliator?
a. A cream to remove superfluous hair.
b. A granular wash which removes dead skin cells.
c. A total sun block cream.

2. Which vitamins are said to help clear up spots?
a. A and B6.
b. C.
c. D and E.

3. Which of the following exercises will help you burn up the calories best?
a. A fast walk.
b. Squash.
c. Horse riding.

4. If you colour your hair with henna, are the results:
a. Semi-permanent?
b. Wash in/wash out?
c. Permanent?

5. Which is the best method for closing open pores?
a. There isn't one.
b. A face pack once a week.
c. A very strong astringent used after cleansing.

6. If you hair's greasy, should you:
a. Leave your hair as long as you can bear it before washing it with a shampoo for greasy hair?
b. Wash every day if you like with a gentle 'baby' or frequent wash shampoo?
c. Wash every three days with a special medicated shampoo?

7. Which of the following ways of brushing your teeth is favoured by most hygienists?
a. Brush from side to side.
b. Brush up and down.
c. Brush in small circles.

8. Should you wash your face:
a. Never?
b. Only if your skin's very oily?
c. If you like?

9. How often should you condition your hair?
a. After every wash.
b. Once a week.
c. Every six weeks.

10. Which is the best way to cover up spots?
a. Don't use make-up on spots, it'll make them worse.
b. Smooth on foundation or cover-up stick a shade lighter than your skin tone.
c. Smooth on foundation or cover-up stick the same colour as your skin tone.

11. It's time to get your nails into shape. Do you:
a. Use nail scissors?
b. Use the fine side of an emery board to file your nails into shape using a see-sawing, side-to-side action?
c. Use the fine side of an emery board to file your nails into shape, moving from the sides into the centre?

12. How often should you get your hair trimmed?
a. Every six weeks.
b. It depends if you're growing it or not.
c. Every three months.

13. What causes spots?
a. Dirt.
b. Hormones.
c. A bad diet.

14. You're about to pluck your eyebrows. Do you:
a. Pluck away stragglers from underneath brows?
b. Pluck hairs from all around your eyebrow?
c. Remove hairs from within the eyebrow?

STUFF

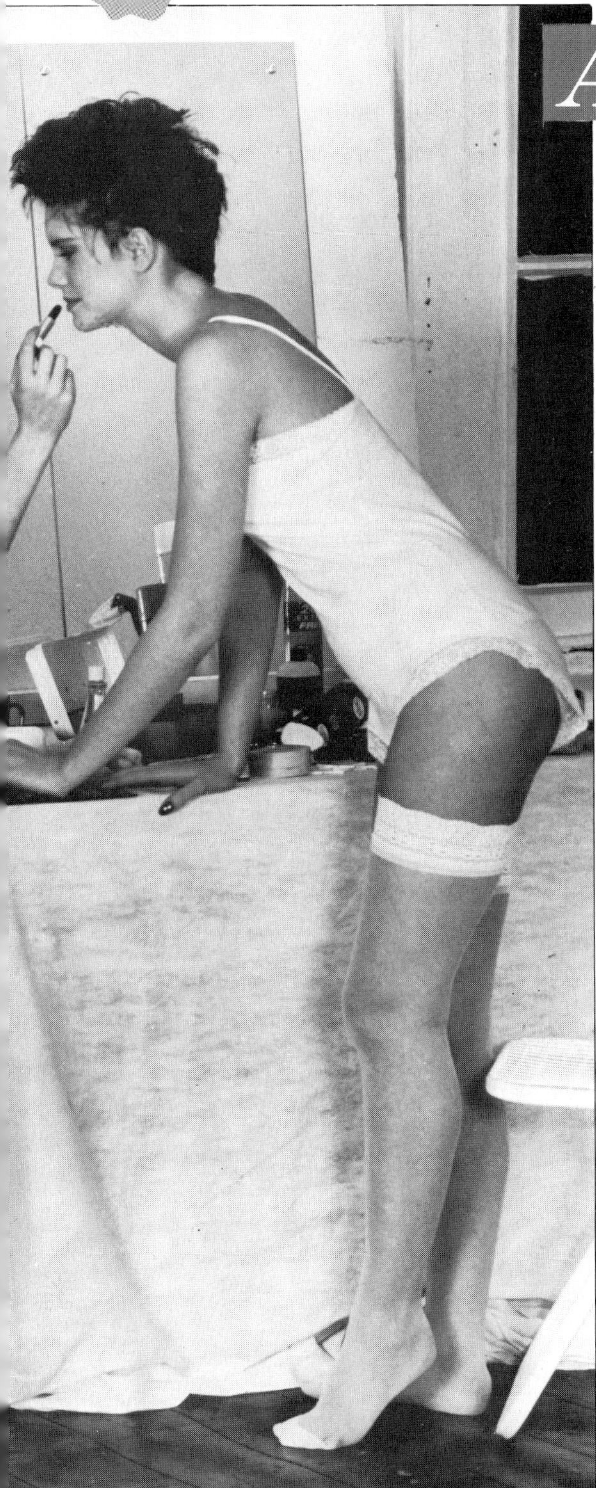

ANSWERS

1.b. An exfoliator is a granular wash which removes dull, greyish dead skin cells, which can clog the sebaceous glands aiding the formation of spots and blackheads, to reveal finer skin.

2.a. Vitamins A and B6 have been linked with spots so make sure you're getting a good supply of these vitamins for clear skin.

3.a. A fast walk burns up the calories best as it is an 'aerobic' form of exercise, raising the heartbeat gently and keeping it at a steady level. Regular exercise of this type will raise the metabolic rate so you burn calories more efficiently even when you're not exercising.

4.c. Henna is a permanent dye, and will not wash out. As it's made from natural ingredients it also conditions the hair beautifully.

5.a. Open pores cannot be closed permanently, although face packs and astringents cause muscles in the skin to contract making the pores seem smaller.

6.b. If your hair's greasy, wash it as often as it needs it, but use a gentle shampoo. A shampoo for greasy hair could aggravate the condition even further if used often, and dry out the ends leading to splitting.

7.c. Most hygienists' favourite method of cleaning the teeth at present is to move the brush in small circles.

8.c. Whether you wash your face or use cotton wool and cleanser is entirely a personal choice. But do use a special facial wash or cleansing bar, and make sure you rinse it off properly as any residue may cause dryness and irritation.

9.a. Whatever your hair type, even if it's blooming with health, it needs conditioning after every wash.

10.b. sing make-up on your face will not cause spots or make them worse. To cover them up, use a cover-up stick or foundation which is a shade lighter than your skin tone. Smooth over the blemish with a fine flat brush and blend in.

11.c. To get your nails into shape, use the fine side of an emery board moving it in one direction only, from the sides into the centre. Do not use scissors, or a see-sawing action, as both can produce rough edges and flaking.

12.a. Our hair should be trimmed every six weeks regardless of whether it's being grown or not. This will keep the style in shape, and prevent and remove split, straggly ends.

13.b. Overactive hormones are responsible for greasy skin and spots. This is why they're so prevalent during teenage years, as hormone levels are changing. Dirt and diet do not cause spots although an imbalanced diet does seem to aggravate them.

14.a. Pluck hairs from underneath your eyebrows only. Retain the natural shape by removing straggly hairs, then brush brows upward and into shape with an old toothbrush.

FATE HAS FOUR VOICES

Blind dates never work out, do they? But sometimes, it's worth giving love a chance...

KEITH

We turned the corner into High Street, Mike and I. He was striding. I was shambling. There was a very definite someone he was striding towards. Beth. And there was a very definite reason for my shambling. Reluctance.

I didn't want to be here. I'd rather have done anything than to be here – taken a trip on a crocodile down the Amazon, been captured by hostile gorillas in Africa, listened to a Black Lace record. Anything.

"Hang on, Keith!" Mike said suddenly, stopping dead in his tracks and putting out his arm sharply like a traffic cop, coming close to breaking a couple of my ribs in the process. "I think that we've got a slight problem here."

"Me?" I asked.

Well, I knew it. I knew it the moment I looked at myself in the mirror, before breaking out in that cold sweat.

Even a blind date would have to be blind to see that I'm not in the same league as Mike. And my taste in clothes leaves something to be desired.

So which problem, specifically, was Mike referring to? My permanent scared-sheep expression, my jeans and sweatshirt outfit – I realised when I saw him coming down the road in his flash Italian suit and his smooth designer shirt that I was all wrong – or was it my general long-legged gawkiness?

"You?" he asked, peering into the distance.

"I'm all wrong. You ought to stop taking pity on me. Look, let's forget about this whole blind date thing. I think I'll just go back home, right? I'm off, see ya!"

"Not you, stupid. That. Look! Look what that lovely Beth's dragged along for you," he sighed, grabbing me as I turned, whirling me round again, and pointing into the gloomy distance where little black specks swam in a grey mist.

"What?" I asked.

"Put your glasses on and cop a load of that!"

"But you said I hadn't to wear my glasses. You said that it puts girls off. You said..."

"Just get them on, and stop arguing! Now, can you see?" he asked, as the mist swam into focus, and two girls crisped into vision.

One girl was Beth. No mistaking her long blonde hair, her elegant cool manner, her eye-boggling beauty. She was the sort of girl who took your breath away.

And the other? The other girl was a kind of...

"A hedgehog in drag!" Mike spat. "Where on earth did Beth dredge *her* up from?"

BETH

I was desperate.

"Please, Katie!" I begged. "Mike asked me to find someone for Keith, just for the evening, and no one was free!"

"So you bump into me at the bus stop, and think you'll make one last effort?" Katie asked, her mouth curved into that disconcerting see-through smile.

"That sort of thing," I admitted.

"I'm your last hope?"

"Yes," I confessed dismally.

Last hope was right. Katie would never have entered my head as a suitable blind date for anyone.

For a start, she had no track record at all, not like Debbie Bird, who'd turned me down flat with a "Him? Keith Waters? I think I'll get more excitement staying home and washing my hair!"

Sal had said, "Sorry, kiddo. Got a big date with Paul Smith tonight," and even spotty Melanie had groaned, "Keith? That grunty guy with the long, skinny legs and the scruffy jeans. No chance".

I had done my best. Now, I was doing my worst. But what choice did I have?

"No," Katie said, quite definitely.

"He's a really nice guy, you know. Honest. He's a bit shy, but ever so interesting when you get to know him, I think. Well, Mike said he is, anyway. He's not bad looking. See! He's just come round the corner now. Please, Katie. Look!"

She didn't even glance over at him. I glanced at Mike. Gorgeous as ever. Smart, smooth, stylish. Then I switched my gaze to Keith. A prune. An absolute prune.

But talking of prunes, Katie was nothing special, especially not at the moment, with her unkempt hair blowing round her face, and that shapeless, woolly bobbled jacket. Maybe when you got to know her... But I never had. She was just a funny kid with a strange smile, and determined ways.

"I've got a bus to catch. I'm going home. Sorry, Beth," she smiled, still watching out for the bus, refusing to look at the boys who were walking towards us.

get this hedgehog in tight focus, eh?"

"Forget it, Mike" he hissed back. "Love me, love my specs, I've decided. Anyway, so far, I'm only getting a close-up of the hair, I want to be in the picture when she turns round."

"Hi, Bethie!" I grinned, taking hold of her hand, and sending disappointed warning signals out through my clenched-up eyes.

We'd been going steady for long

MIKE

"Look. I'm sorry I got you into this, Keith," I muttered. "But try to get through the evening somehow. I just can't believe it! Beth said she'd fix you up with Debbie, or Sal, or maybe Mel..."

"What? The Three Witches?!" Keith groaned. "You were going to get me a date with one of the Three Witches? Good job you didn't tell me that, I'd never've bothered to come at all. I'd never've bothered to get all dressed up!"

I gave him a quick glance, to see whether he was joking or serious. You never could tell with Keith. His sarcastic sense of humour sometimes caught me on the hop. He was a funny, deep guy. I liked him. Thousands didn't.

"You can take your glasses off now!" I hissed as we drew close. "Better not

enough for my message to come over loud and clear.

I wanted her to know that I wasn't too pleased about the arrangements. Not at all.

"Oh, hi, Mike!" she replied, falsely bright and loud, and sending flashing messages back.

"Keith... Sorry. I really am. Deb was coming, but she broke her ankle as we were walking down her front path. She sends her apologies, and says she hopes to meet you soon, when she's recovered!"

"So, who's..." I whispered, nudging my thumb towards the cloud of blue-black hair and the back of the bobbly jacket.

"Katie Doran. She's just waiting for a bus," Beth mouthed. "She'd be no use, anyway."

"Well..." I sighed, all deflated.

Keith shrugged, and smiled. The smile was a real beam of pleasure and relief.

"I'll get the next bus then. Thanks, Beth. You don't know how much I appreciate this!" he laughed. "Go on, then, you two. Don't let me keep you. I'm okay!"

"Sure? I asked, guiltily.

"Sure!" he said. He looked as if he meant it, too. I took hold of Beth's hand, and walked her away, towards the disco. Keith stood at the bus stop, whistling to himself and tapping one foot. I'd let him down. So why did he look so happy?

"He's deep," I told Beth.

"Glad he's got something going for him," Beth grumbled.

KATIE

I turned round, in response to the tune some guy was whistling behind my back. And then my heart skipped first one beat, then the next. I laughed to cover it up.

"It's you! Thought I recognised the whistle!"

"I knew it was you. I recognised your hair," he grinned.

It was a beautiful smile. And a haunting tune. I'd tumbled into both, once before. I'd been sitting in the front row at the folk club, when he had got up to sing.

His song had been different from all the others, a sad, lilting love song, that he'd written himself. And, as he'd sung, that night, his eyes had rested on me gently, until I was singing, too, inside. Then Paula had said, "We'll miss the last bus if we don't leave now," and I hadn't had time to wait for the applause to die down before I was pulled out through the crowds, away from him.

"I wanted to talk to you last Wednesday," I told him. "Only..."

"Yeah. Saw you leaving. D'you go to the club much?" he asked.

"First time..." I stammered. I couldn't stop looking at him, staring. like some stupid, half-baked kid.

"Shall we go now?" he asked.

"Why not," I said.

He held out his hand for me. Mine fitted inside it, snug and warm, as if that's where it belonged.

I hoped it did anyway.

MY GUY LOVE STORY

WHEN THE CHIPS

Are you facing a crisis point? Fed up with feeling podgy, out-of-puff and pale-faced? Well, we've got the answers to help you start afresh with a healthy body, a slimline figure . . . and we might even let you bite into a few French fries!

CRASH DIETS

I'm really fat and I hate diets. I find the best way to lose weight is to go on a crash diet for about a week. The only problem is that I put weight back on again really quickly. Have you any advice?

Tracey, Nottingham.

The most important piece of advice I can give you is to tell you to stop going on crash diets. Trying to lose weight in this way can be very dangerous. Your body needs a regular supply of protein, vitamins and minerals in order to function properly, and to keep you fit and healthy – especially when you are in your teens and still developing. You should never allow yourself to feel hungry when you are on a diet, or miss out on main meals.

The most sensible way to lose weight is not to eat less but to change the way you eat. Here are a few simple guidelines:

* Cut down on fried and fatty food (grill food instead)
* Eat less red meat (it has a high fat content)
* Eat more chicken (trim off any fat) and fish
* Cut down on high-fat dairy products (stick to low-fat cheeses, such as cottage cheese, Edam and Brie; substitute skimmed or semi-skimmed milk for ordinary silver top; and eat plenty of natural yoghurt)
* Spread margarine or butter very thinly
* Eat plenty of fresh fruit, vegetables and salad
* Cut down on sugar, sweets, biscuits, cakes, etc.

Once you start applying these few simple rules every day and think very carefully about what you are eating, you should find that you'll lose those extra pounds and you'll be feeling much healthier too!

JUNK FOOD

I love junk food, especially hamburgers, chips and chocolate. But my mum says that it's not good for me. I never feel ill and I have quite a good figure, so I don't know what she's going on about.

Lindsey, Croydon.

There's been a lot of research into "fast food" to test whether it's bad for people. Basically, as long as you're following a well-balanced, varied diet which is made up from fresh and unprocessed foods, there is no harm in having the odd hamburger or bar of chocolate. In fact, that old favourite, a plate of fish and chips will do you a lot of good – but it will also be very high in calories!

You sound quite fit so you must be getting your fair share of nutrients, and you are probably one of those very lucky people who can eat whatever they like and not worry about putting on weight!

However, there's just a couple of points to bear in mind: always eat what your mother prepares for you, and don't skip meals then stuff yourself with packets of crisps and other junk-type food.

WORK OUT

Please help, I'm really fed up. I've tried several different diets but I just can't seem to lose weight – I lose a couple of pounds but that's about

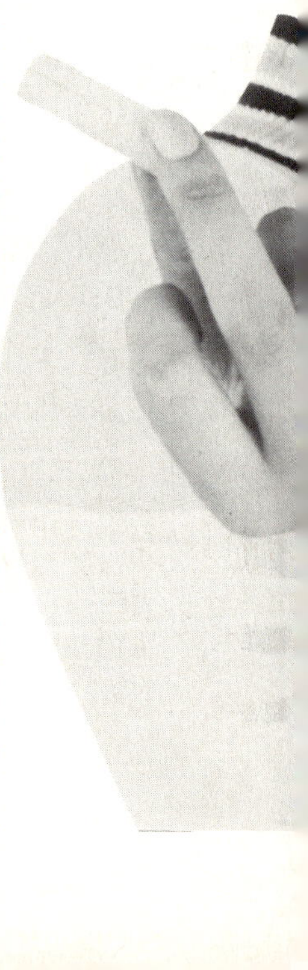

ARE DOWN!

all. I always follow a diet properly and I never cheat. What can I do now?

Sally, Liverpool.

There could be several reasons why you are finding it difficult to lose weight. One reason may be that you don't really need to lose any weight – you may have reached a sort of "plateau".

I suggest you see your doctor and ask him or her the correct weight for your size, shape and age.

If your doctor thinks that you are overweight, he or she will give you a medically approved diet sheet, and advice about how to lose weight. Alternatively, you could contact Weight Watchers (phone 01-834 9090 for details of your local branch). They offer much help, support and sensible advice on slimming, and their diet has a high success rate.

Another reason could be that you've taken on a bit of puppy fat.

This is very common in teenage girls and is all part of the developing process.

Puppy fat is quite difficult to shift but it will disappear as you get older and your body changes.

It could also be possible that you have a low metabolism – you don't burn up food very quickly. And one way to combat that is to take up a regular exercise such as swimming, jogging and aerobics.

Exercise is very important because not only does it keep you fit, but it helps you relax, it tones up your muscles so you don't feel so flabby, and it helps burn up those extra troublesome calories at a much faster rate.

Quite often, following a diet is not enough, you've got to move that body and work off a few pounds too!

Clare
"Can I do some dedications?"
YOU SAID YOU'D GO SWIMMING, YOU CAN'T BACK OUT NOW.
WHY DON'T YOU COME, CLARE?
I HATE GETTING MY HAIR WET, IT TAKES AGES TO DRY.
AND YOU GET IT FULL OF CHLORINE.
I WISH YOU'D HAVE TOLD US BEFORE, WE COULD HAVE ASKED SOMEONE ELSE.
SO YOU'RE NOT COMING?
THAT IS THE IDEA WHEN I SAY NO.
COME ON, SANDRA, LEAVE HER. SHE'LL BE SORRY SHE DIDN'T COME, YOU WAIT. WE MIGHT MEET SOME REALLY INTERESTING GUYS.
Later on that day.
CLARE, PHONE!
CLARE THOMAS?
HELLO.
YES.
THIS IS RADIO WOODSIDE, YOUR INDEPENDENT LOCAL RADIO STATION.
YOUR DETAILS HAVE BEEN SENT IN BY JULIE THORPE. SHE'S ENTERED YOU IN OUR FIVE DAY CHALLENGE. THE QU WHERE WE ASK YOU A QUESTIO A DAY AND AT THE END OF THI WEEK, THERE'S A BIG PRIZE WAITING.

ARE YOU READY, CLARE?
ER. . .YES, I THINK SO.
GOOD. NOW, WHO DESIGNED ST PAUL'S CATHEDRAL?. . .AND I MUST TAKE YOUR FIRST ANSWER.
CHRISTOPHER WREN.
IS CORRECT, CONGRATULATIONS, YOU'RE THROUGH DAY ONE OF THE FIVE DAY CHALLENGE. WE'LL SPEAK TO YOU TOMORROW.
CLARE! CLARE! I JUST HEARD YOU ON THE RADIO!
WHAT WAS IT LIKE? YOU DIDN'T SOUND NERVOUS.
THAT'S 'COS I WASN'T EXPECTING IT TO HAPPEN.
DID YOU KNOW THAT THE PRIZE IF YOU WIN THROUGH ALL FIVE DAYS IS A HOLIDAY IN PARIS?
HOLIDAY IN PARIS? I THOUGHT IT'D BE SOME CRUMMY RADIO WOODSIDE SWEATSHIRT OR A £2 RECORD TOKEN.
NO, IT'S THE BIZ. YOU'VE GOT TO DO A DEDICATION FOR ME TOMORROW TOO. YOU WILL, WON'T YOU?
Clare couldn't wait to see Julie and tell her about the quiz.
. . .ANYWAY, THANKS FOR ENTERING ME IN IT.
THAT'S ALRIGHT, I SENT THE CARD OFF YEARS AGO. I'D FORGOTTEN ABOUT IT ALTOGETHER.
IF I'D HAVE GONE SWIMMING, I'D HAVE MISSED IT. YOU SEE HOW RIGHT I WAS ABOUT NOT GOING.
MMM, THAT IS A LUCKY BREAK, ISN'T IT, MARTIN?
CERTAINLY SOUNDS LIKE IT?
WILL YOU COME AND HELP ME TOMORROW?

OH, I DON'T KNOW, ISN'T THAT AGAINST THE RULES?
EVERYBODY DOES IT. YOU ALWAYS HEAR PEOPLE IN THE BACKGROUND ON RADIO QUIZZES GIVING THEM HELP.
ALRIGHT, THEN.
So, the next day.
WHAT HAVE YOU GOT THAT LOT FOR?
THIS IS JUST IN CASE I CAN'T THINK OF THE ANSWER STRAIGHT AWAY. THEY'RE ENCYCLOPEDIAS, YOU CAN FIND THINGS REALLY QUICKLY.
HELLO, CLARE, DAY TWO. NERVOUS?
A LITTLE BIT.
ALRIGHT, WHAT WAS WHAM!'S FIRST NUMBER ONE SINGLE?
UM. . .ER. . .OH, I SHOULD KNOW THIS. . .
WHY CAN'T I THINK OF IT?
WAKE ME UP BEFORE YOU GO GO.
YES, YOU'VE GOT IT.WELL DONE.
THANKS, JOOLS. I KNEW THE ANSWER, THEN. I JUST COULDN'T THINK OF IT. I'LL HAVE TO REMEMBER TO BUY A COPY OF THE GUINNESS BOOK OF BRITISH HIT SINGLES.
THAT'S THE ANSWER I WAS LOOKING FOR, CLARE, WELL DONE.THREE IN A ROW!
CAN I DO SOME DEDICATIONS?TO JULIE, SANDRA, DONNA, MUM AND ARTHUR, CHERYL, DEIDRE. . .
THANK YOU, WE HAVE GOT A PROGRAMME TO RUN, YOU KNOW.

Day Four and Clare was getting a bigger and bigger audience.
WHICH IS THE TALLEST BUILDING IN LONDON?
THE NATWEST TOWER.
THE NATWEST TOWER.
YES, YOU'RE RIGHT.
Friday came around. It was time for the big one.
CLARE, CAN YOU TELL HOW MANY O–LEVELS YOUR FRIEND JULIE THORPE HAS GOT?
WHAT? – ER, SHE'S GOT SEVEN.
THAT WAS EASY, I DIDN'T EVEN NEED ANY HELP.
CONGRATULATIONS, YOU'VE JUST WON THE BIGGY!
ACTUALLY, IT'S MARTIN, CLARE.
MARTIN? MARTIN WHAT ARE YOU DOING ON THE PHONE, GET OFF! THE GUY FROM RADIO WOODSIDE'S TRYING TO GET THROUGH.
NO, HE'S NOT. IT WAS ME ALL ALONG.
DON'T BLAME ME, JULIE MADE ME DO IT, SHE SAID YOU'D BE GAME FOR A LAUGH. WE SET IT UP THAT AFTERNOON YOU WERE SUPPOSED TO GO SWIMMING WITH THEM.
AND I FELL FOR IT, HOOK, LINE AND SINKER.
WERE YOU ALL IN ON THIS?
'FRAID SO.
SO WHEN YOU CAME ROUND AND SAID 'I JUST HEARD YOU ON THE RADIO' THAT WAS ALL AN ACT?
DO I GET AN OSCAR?
GO ON, SAY IT, CLARE, IT'LL MAKE YOU FEEL BETTER.
YOU B......!
Clare wasn't going to live this one down in a hurry!

IF YOU'VE

Every week on My Guy our postbag is full of letters asking for advice. Here are a few of the problems that crop up more than most…

SHE'S EMBARRASSING

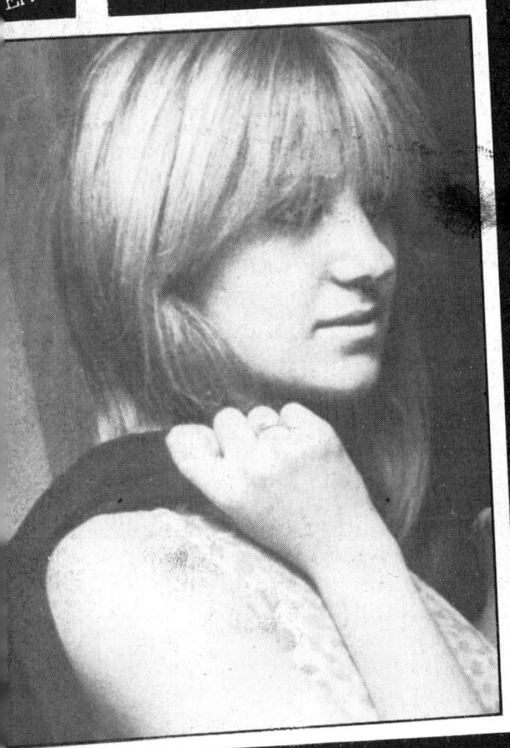

Our problem is one of our friends. She dresses funnily. It has got to the stage where we feel embarrassed walking along beside her as everyone stares, makes comments or bursts out laughing. She wears old-fashioned trousers and jumpers or else her school clothes. And it isn't that she is poor. She is just stubborn and won't do anything to change her appearance. How can we get her to take more interest in clothes and dress differently without hurting her feelings even more? Please help us.

Embarrassed FGTH Fans

I'm sure that you must both be exaggerating about the reactions of people in the street to the way your friend dresses.

Since reading your letter I've looked out particularly for unfashionably dressed teenagers and watched reactions. And most people don't notice at all!

I think that if your friend is taking little or no interest in her personal appearance, and it sounds that way, there can only be one or two explanations. One is that she thinks it completely unimportant and if so, you should respect her views about that. The other is that she has little self-value. And criticizing her won't help that! Complimenting her will!

Telling her you've seen some super jeans that you're sure she'd look great in is far more likely to boost her self-confidence and encourage her to take a pride in herself, than any amount of negative comments.

Be gentle and be patient.

ASK HIM YOURSELF

I have wanted to go out with this boy Tony for ages. My cousin asked him if he would go out with me but I am still waiting for his answer. What do you think I should do? Ask him myself, or leave it?

Sister Sledge Fan, Kilmarnock.

If you've liked him for all that time, you might as well ask him yourself and see what he says.

I never think it is a good idea to ask others to do it for you – the person concerned has no way of knowing whether the offer is a serious one, or just a joke.

Even if he refuses you, at least you will have tried, and it may help you to get him out of your system.

And you never know what will happen – he just may say yes!!

INJECTION FEAR

I have to have a rubella injection at school soon and I am really scared. Some people say it hurts and I get so scared about it that once I fainted. I sometimes wonder if I should have it done. What do you think?

Worried Wham Fan, Middlesex.

Yes, I think you should have it done. It will hurt a little bit – all injections do. But it is over in a couple of seconds – unlike the emotional pain of having a baby born handicapped as a result of a rubella infection. That pain lasts a lifetime. If you are nervous, it might be a good idea for you to have your injection at your family doctor's. I think that when a lot of girls are done at once at school, it can cause a bit of hysteria among the more sensitive ones. Talk to your mum about it.